# Children of the
# FOREST

**DANCING PYGMY.**
Egyptian sculpture.
Ivory.
From Lisht-Tomb of Hepy.
Twelfth Dynasty
(About 2000 B.C.)
The Metropolitan Museum of Art,
Museum Excavations, 1933–1934;
　Rogers Fund, 1934.

KEVIN DUFFY

# Children of the
# FOREST

DODD, MEAD & COMPANY
NEW YORK

TO ALL YOU BAMBUTI WHEREVER YOU ARE. . . .

AND TO GERLINDE, WITHOUT WHOM THIS BOOK

WOULD NOT HAVE BEEN WRITTEN.

Copyright © 1984 by Kevin Duffy
All rights reserved
No part of this book may be reproduced in any form
without permission in writing from the publisher.
Published by Dodd, Mead & Company, Inc.
79 Madison Avenue, New York, N.Y. 10016
Distributed in Canada by
McClelland and Stewart Limited, Toronto
Manufactured in the United States of America
Designed by G. G. Laurens
First Edition

Library of Congress Cataloging in Publication Data
Duffy, Kevin.
  Children of the forest.
  I. Bambute.  I. Title.
DT650.B36D84  1984      306'.08996      84-10239
ISBN 0-396-08430-3

# CONTENTS

*Illustrations appear on pages 25-30, 71-76, 109-114, and 150-155.*

# PREFACE

$\curlyvee$

Try to imagine a way of life where land, shelter, and food are free, and where there are no leaders, bosses, politics, organized crime, taxes, or laws. Add to this the benefits of being part of a society where everything is shared, where there are no rich people and no poor people, and where happiness does not mean the accumulation of material possessions. Put all this together and you have part of the traditional life of Africa's hunting and gathering Mbuti Pygmies who live in the Ituri forest of Zaire. The life includes—for about four hours of work per day—a steady supply of food, along with good fellowship, music, dancing, singing, and a pride and pleasure in one's family. For those so inclined, free love is openly enjoyed and even ritualized among the young people, yet marriage, when it occurs, is generally monogamous and permanent.

Before you decide to pack your bags and relocate to Zaire's Ituri forest, it may be important to know that this apparent Utopia does not include the modern benefits of piped-in water, electricity, medical care (except for natural remedies), or comfortably furnished homes where privacy for the individual is assured. Such things are not easily available if you must walk miles with your total possessions to a new location every few weeks, as the nomadic Mbuti Pygmies do. The only home they know is a one-room, beehive-shaped structure made in about two hours from sticks and leaves. It has no window or door and is barely the length of a sleeping person. Only a child could stand upright inside. The Mbuti have never learned to make any other kind of shelter.

Stone toolmaking began in East Africa about 2.5 million years ago. Yet there is no evidence that the Mbuti—or any other

African rain forest Pygmies—ever made stone tools or weapons. Indeed the Mbuti are an essentially prehistoric group of hunters and gatherers who survived into the twentieth century without ever learning to work with clay, stone, or metal. They still use wooden-tipped arrows unless given metal ones by other tribes. As nomads they have never domesticated animals or planted crops. To this day they have never learned to make fire and must carry it with them from camp to camp.

There are many possible reasons why the Mbuti did not become more "advanced" in the past thousands of years. There may not have been a readily available supply of stones in the forest that flaked easily into tools, or from which they could have smelted iron. There were probably no seasonal starvation periods and no ice ages to stimulate innovative ideas or changes in techniques. It is likely that for millennia they were the only human beings in the forest and therefore never had occasion to develop weapons of war or fortified communities.

Perhaps long ago the Mbuti decided that they had everything they wanted, and that to have more was undesirable. To this day a nomadic Mbuti band will publicly criticize one of their own who hoards or keeps something to himself that the others don't have. In the same way there are no chiefs among the Mbuti because to be chief means to have power that others do not have. An informal system of community approval—or disapproval—takes the place of laws or kingly authority. Whatever the reasons, the Mbuti culture adequately survived through the centuries, while the great civilizations of ancient Egypt, Greece, and Rome rose and fell.

At a time when our own civilization threatens to destroy the planet earth, it is gratifying to witness occasional signs that the simple ways of the past are still appreciated, and indeed are sometimes more effective than the new.

When the United States sent a plaque into outer space with a message to the beings who might possibly find it, we had in part reverted back to the style of our cave-painting, paleolithic ancestors. In a friendly introduction of ourselves to whoever might be out there, we inscribed on the plaque the outlines of a male and female of our species. In a down-to-earth manner both were naked. The man's penis and the woman's breasts just might be more clearly understood than any written language. The Mbuti might not have invented the steam engine, but perhaps in the quiet solitude of their forest home they, too, discovered that less is more.

This book describes my experiences among the extraordinary Mbuti Pygmies who are living in the distant past today. Through it the reader can share their friendship and perhaps envy their freedom. It does not explain the continuing mystery of their ancient origin.

# Children of the
# FOREST

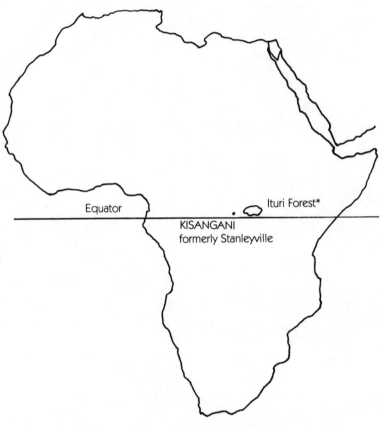

Equator

Ituri Forest*

KISANGANI
formerly Stanleyville

*Location of Mbuti Pygmies

# 1

---

## The Place, The People

Forbidding and mysterious to those who see it for the first time, and even to some who live in it, the Ituri rain forest lies a half-degree north of the equator in the center of the African continent. Today part of the nation of Zaire, this forest is still one of the most inaccessible places in Africa. In addition, it is the home of the smallest people on earth, the Mbuti Pygmies.

Only one major road cuts east to west through the Ituri forest's fifty thousand square miles. Built in the early 1930s, the road has degenerated for much of its length into a muddy track only wide enough for one vehicle, which makes for interesting encounters when the traveler meets oncoming traffic. At best, the road surface is simply the flattened earth left when the trees were cleared. At its worst, the way becomes a seemingly endless nightmare of treacherous mud dotted here and there with helpless vehicles bogged down for days and sometimes longer. And always the primeval forest looms over the road, forever waiting to take back this puny man-made strip, which scars the ancient landscape.

I had just survived the rigors of this road in order to reach the village of Epulu. Such villages in the Ituri are populated mainly by tribal Bantu or Sudanic Negro farmers who migrated into the forest in relatively recent times. It was my third expedition into this remote region in ten years to study the nomadic Mbuti Pygmies, thought by some scholars to have been the original inhabitants of the region. I had previously made a documentary film about them, *Pygmies of the Rain Forest* (which was broadcast as *BaMiki BaNdula—Children of the Forest* on the Nova TV series). I was in the area a third time, as I had just concluded an official expedition into the Ituri on behalf of the Los Angeles County Museum of Natural History. My obligations to the museum fulfilled, my time was now my own, and I was free to wander into the forest to find a hunting band of nomadic Mbuti Pygmies.

Just who were the Mbuti that I had come to visit?

They collectively call themselves *Bambuti,* and they are probably the largest and culturally purest group of Pygmy hunters and gatherers in the forests of equatorial Africa. Nobody knows how many there are, and estimates have varied from 20,000 to 50,000. My personal estimate of the total number of relatively unacculturated Mbuti today is 20,000. In the Ituri forest—excluding permanent roadside settlements—that would mean a Mbuti population density of less than one Pygmy to a square mile. In New York's Manhattan, there are about 77,000 people per square mile. To an Mbuti in his majestic primeval forest, such numbers would be nightmarish, like changing all the trees into people, which may in fact be how the Manhattan Indians felt after they saw their island settled by the European hordes.

Except for a few stone implements associated with gold workings, there have been no Stone Age artifacts found anywhere in the Ituri forest, the place where the Mbuti are thought to have lived in isolation for thousands of years. Until regular contact was established with other tribes, these nomadic hunters and gatherers have never known the benefits of farming or the use of iron tools.

Although they knew nothing of these things—or because they didn't—they are as biologically well adapted to the forest as the birds and the antelope. In their long history, they have never harmed their environment or threatened the existence of a single animal or plant species.

They are also probably more culturally integrated with their environment than any other group of hunters and gatherers has been. Although they work hard enough for the sustenance it provides, they gratefully acknowledge that their beloved forest home gives them everything they need: food, clothing, shelter—and affection. They look on the forest as their parents, as both their father and mother. They sing and pray to it and call themselves its children—the "children of the forest."

Then there are those Negro villagers (including two of the more important groups, the Bantu Bila, or Bira, and the Sudanic Lese) considered recent arrivals because they apparently settled in the forest within only the last few hundred years. They are subsistence farmers, most of whom occupy relatively tiny clearings dotted occasionally along the unpaved, earthen road. For the past couple of generations they have seldom ventured into the vast primary forest, the traditional home of the Mbuti Pygmies, some parts of which are still uninhabited by any human presence at all. Yet a few of the Lese, and probably some of the Bila, have in recent years moved back to ancestral village sites in the depths of the forest, away from the road, which has greatly deteriorated and become less used since independence from Belgian colonial rule. They have found what the Mbuti have known for years—that the forest is a good place in which to escape from government officials and other less attractive aspects of civilization in the relatively urban life of a mixed, roadside community where kinship and other traditional values are eroded.

There are two main groups of nomadic Pygmies living in the Ituri forest, the Efe who associate with the Lese and Mamvu cultivators in the northern and eastern regions, and the most studied and perhaps largest group, the Mbuti who occupy the central and southern parts of the forest and who associate with the Bila cultivators. The smaller Aka and Sua Pygmy groups associate with the Mangbetu and Budu tribes respectively. Each Pygmy group speaks a different language from the others, all possibly adopted from their village neighbors.

The Mbuti of the central and southern forest hunt for small antelopes using nets. The Efe Mbuti hunt with the bow and arrow and the basenji hunting dog. The spear is used by all groups when hunting the larger animals, especially the forest buffalo, the okapi, and the elephant.

It is my intention here to examine and compare both the Efe and the Bila Mbuti Pygmies—the archers and the net hunters—and also to explain the relationship between the Mbuti and their "owners," the village cultivators who now share the forest with them.

On previous visits to the Ituri, I had camped in the forest with the more eastern Efe Mbuti—the archers—and it was to them I would return within the year on yet another expedition. But now, here at the village of Epulu, was an opportunity for me to locate and camp with a band of Mbuti who hunt the forest antelope with nets.

In the village of Epulu I soon found an Mbuti named Abeli who would take me northeast into the forest to a hunting camp called Ekale, about six hours' walk away. When I told him that I would need some of my things carried into the forest, Abeli recruited another Mbuti Pygmy named Kachelewa for this task. Apparently Abeli considered it beneath his dignity to carry anything. Kachelewa in turn recruited his wife Anziani to carry for him, for he considered carrying to be a woman's work, especially in the outside world of the villagers.

Abeli looked at me curiously. "How long will you stay in the forest?" he asked in Kingwana, the forest's lingua franca.

I glanced over my rather limited supplies. "Maybe seven days," I told him in the same tongue. "Perhaps less if you and your friends eat all my rice," I added jokingly.

Abeli smiled, lifting my bag of this staple food to test it for himself.

"This is enough rice for everybody," he said, "and besides, there will be much meat in the forest where we are going."

He may have been only about four feet eight inches tall against my five feet ten, but it certainly had no effect on his self-confidence. I decided we would probably get along fine.

On our way into the forest the next morning, we passed through the villagers' gardens, where papaya, sweet potatoes, cassava, pineapples, plantains, and bananas grew all year long in the hot, humid climate of the tropics. These cultivated trees and plants sprouted freely among the scattered remains of the original trees of the forest, which had been felled and burned to make way for the gardens. But the cultivations of the villagers were still only a dot in the wilderness, surrounded by the ever-present, brooding wall of the uncut forest. We reached the forest moments later, our tiny figures suddenly dwarfed by towering trees as we disappeared like ants into its depths.

As we left the sunlight, the temperature abruptly dropped from hot to cool and the sounds of the outside world totally ceased. Instead, there was an eerie silence, sometimes broken by crickets, monkeys, parrots, chimpanzees, hornbills, and very occasionally the trumpeting of an elephant or the cough of a prowling leopard. Nearly a hundred feet above our heads, the treetops joined to form an almost unbroken canopy in all directions, leaving us in a perpetual green twilight. Each tree, magnificently tall, competed with its neighbors in trying to reach the sunlight above. Branches did not form until the canopy level, and so the forest, from our human perspective, was a kind of underworld beneath a high, leafy dome supported by giant pillars. To the Mbuti, introducing the sound of machinery here would be as sacrilegious as starting up a jackhammer in a cathedral. They hate unnecessary noise and think of the forest as sacred.

This is the natural home of the Mbuti Pygmies, a botanical wonderland unchanged for unknown millennia, a place where the Bantu and Sudanic villagers believe the spirits of their ancestors dwell after death.

Here one will not find the ordinary animals commonly identified with Africa—lions, giraffes, zebras, or vast herds of grazing antelope. Instead, there are extraordinary and rarely seen animals such as the okapi, the bongo, the Congo peacock, the giant forest hog, and probably many other species yet unknown to science.

In addition to the common honeybee, the Pygmies know many

different kinds of small stingless bees, some say fifteen different kinds. Any form of honey they produce is of demanding interest to any Mbuti who discovers its presence, and my present companions were no exception.

Ahead of me, Abeli and Kachelewa stopped in their tracks to stare up at a wild bees' nest they had just spotted in a tree above. Anziani paused with them only a moment before impatiently squeezing past on the narrow track to continue the walk alone. She carried the only heavy load and could not be blamed for wanting to reach her destination as soon as possible. And besides, climbing for honey was a man's work.

I too was anxious to reach the hunting camp they called Ekale, and quickly followed behind Anziani. It was not the first time I had found myself being expertly led by a Pygmy woman through the forest wilderness, where an outsider can get lost within minutes. Soon we had left Abeli and Kachelewa far behind as we walked at a steady pace toward Ekale.

When it has been raining, which is often, there is no rush among the Mbuti to take the lead when walking through the forest because the person in front catches most of the moisture that clings to the forest-floor vegetation. The first one to brush against a leafy plant releases on himself a shower of water cooled in the sunless interior of the forest. The second person receives less, and so on down the line until the last person can pass through relatively dry.

Anziani continued her leading role with hardly a pause in her determined stride. Now well into the forest and away from the scornful eyes of the villagers, she put down the heavy basket she carried on her back, which contained, among other things, fifteen kilos of rice and a bunch of fifty bananas. Then, with a careless movement, she removed the cloth wraparound that had covered her body from her breasts to her knees. Underneath, she wore only a narrow piece of bark cloth in traditional Mbuti fashion: a kind of G-string, it was worn between the legs and pulled up front and back and tucked under a slender belt of artistically woven natural fibers.

If society demanded the wearing of something, it was the

ideal way to exist in temperatures that seldom fall below 72 degrees, and where the humidity reaches 100 percent. Both men and women wear the same garment, no more and no less, an original unisex style that the Mbuti had probably invented for themselves. Now as we continued on our way, my guide had an advantage over me. While drops of water simply ran off her bare skin, my clothes would retain the moisture and remain wet and soggy for hours.

In the traditional manner that all Mbuti women use to carry loads, the basket Anziani carried on her back was substantially supported from her head by a strap of bark fiber. Anything balanced directly on the head would not survive for more than a few minutes in the frequent areas of low-hanging foliage. Indeed, some of the antelope trails through the forest are almost tunnellike, requiring that a tall man adopt a chimpanzeelike gait to make any progress. It is in these situations that the Pygmies are glad they are not big and clumsy like the Bantu and European people who sometimes visit their home.

The distant thunder we had heard earlier suddenly sounded much closer, and the filtered sunlight quickly turned to gloom. I knew then it soon wouldn't matter how wet my clothes were. There was a rainstorm coming our way, the kind of torrential downpour that can flood an area in minutes.

I watched Anziani's bare feet nimbly pick their way along the obstacle-ridden track. Even with her heavy load, she kept up a fast pace. I counted her footsteps and found there were 128 in one minute, against my 112. She was only about four and a half feet tall but gave the impression of being able to challenge anything in the forest and win. About twenty-five years old, she had skin the rich color of polished copper and was unusually pretty, with a ready smile that exposed perfect teeth. Her firm breasts showed that she may not have had children, and I idly wondered why, for the Mbuti love children more than anything else in the world.

Suddenly the wind came that often precedes an imminent storm. It bent the tops of even the strongest trees and reached down to pluck at us fragile earthlings on the forest floor. Somewhere a tree or heavy branch splintered and crashed to the ground. And ever closer came the lightning bolts, terrifying in their random selection of targets.

Then the rain started, gently at first, but becoming heavier each moment. It was noon, yet the light reaching the forest floor through a rare patch of open sky was like the final moment before nightfall. A tongue of lightning seared its way through the rain to burn and shatter a nearby tree, shaking the earth with its deafening thunder. I wanted to run for shelter, but there was nowhere to run. Shielding my eyes, I peered ahead and was greatly relieved to see Anziani waiting just ahead, the rain dancing against her coppery skin. I saw her lips moving, but whatever she said was lost in a clap of thunder. She beckoned with her arm and I followed her into a mossy shelter formed by the buttress roots of a giant tree. Any previous social inhibitions we may have had were forgotten in the common need to take shelter. I helped remove the heavy load from her back, and we snuggled together as far into the tree as we could go.

In twenty-five years in the African bush, I had experienced it all many times before—the blinding rain, the swollen streams and rivers, the dragging mud, the sense of utter isolation, the helplessness in the face of possible illness, injury, or death. The lightning striking all around and sometimes killing, was challenging, exhilarating, and frightening.

I stayed in the shelter of the tree with Anziani until the heavy rain stopped and we heard Abeli and Kachelewa approaching. Apparently they had failed to reach the honey, but the delay had saved them a drenching, for the rain had missed them almost entirely. I helped Anziani with her basket, and soon we were all once more on the march, with Anziani again leading the way. Now she wielded a leafy branch with which she shook off excess moisture from the foliage ahead. But it made little difference, for the forest canopy would drip on us for hours like light rain.

It was fascinating to speculate on the Mbuti's remarkable sense of direction. There was never a horizon to take a bearing on. The position of the sun was often totally obscured by clouds or a dense canopy of trees. The tracks these people followed were often meandering game trails. Yet the Mbuti always knew where they were going.

To wander through the primeval Ituri forest in the twentieth century in search of a band of nomadic Pygmies is comparable to entering a time machine and wishing myself ten thousand years back in time. To actually find such a band is the fulfillment of such a fantasy. When we approached Ekale late that afternoon, Abeli stopped and cocked his head, listening. For hours we had been walking away from the known world and penetrating deeper into the heart of a seemingly unpopulated, primordial forest. Yet the sound that now floated faintly through the trees ahead was the unmistakable lilt of human voices. They had a tinkling, musical quality, and it was easy to imagine the sound to be an illusion, a trick of the mind in the lonely isolation of the forest. But the voices were real and a most welcome sound to the ears of a tired traveler.

The first glimpse of Ekale was of two little beehive-shaped dwellings no more than four and a half feet high. On going closer, I saw that there were twenty-one huts altogether in a rough circle among the trees. Made of saplings and covered with leaves, they were an organic part of the forest, and it would have been possible to pass just a few yards away and not know they were there.

Little children played outside one of the huts, and two women and an old man were sitting at a fire. Two other women carrying bundles of firewood were just walking into the camp from a direction opposite us. The adults wore the traditional piece of bark cloth, and the two younger women had their legs and faces painted.

Meat racks outside several of the huts were laden with the carcasses of various kinds of small antelopes drying in the smoke from fires beneath. Large leaves covering the carcasses kept the smoke circulating around the meat and also formed a roof to protect the fires from rain. The hard work of previous days had evidently resulted in a surplus of meat, which could be bartered with the village cultivators for bananas, cassava, peanuts, and perhaps even a little bangi—known elsewhere as cannabis sativa, or marijuana.

As I materialized out of the forest, one of the children looked up and ran screaming into its mother's arms and the others bolted into the nearest hut. The adults quickly recognized my companions, to whom they were related, and replied to my greetings with a reserved courtesy. They were astonished to see me walk out of the forest but soon accepted me well enough, as indeed they would anybody in need of a place to stay for the night. There was no other human community within walking distance before nightfall, and they knew this better than I.

Abeli and Kachelewa joined me at the fire with the old man, where I watched his wife making twine for a hunting net by rolling strands of bark from the kusa vine with her hands against her bare thigh. We were told that almost everybody from the camp was in the forest, hunting with the nets, and they would all be back soon. I also discovered it was a time of the *Molimo* in Ekale, a kind of religious festival that was bound to make my stay even more interesting. After a polite interval, I inquired about having a hut built for me, as it would be dark in a couple of hours. Abeli agreed and soon arranged with a woman relative named Sangali to build my new hut.

The only problem was where. I politely rejected a too prominent spot in the center of the camp and pointed to an empty space between two huts. It was on low ground, with a chance of being flooded in heavy rain, but it was the only site left that would not place me too far in or out of the social circle. I was already so very different as a *Muzungu*, or European, and did not want to stand out even more by having my hut built in a place eccentric to traditional ways.

It was getting late, and starting from the bare ground, Sangali had only about two hours to build a hut for me—or less if a distant thunderstorm came our way before nightfall. She began by collecting bundles of freshly cut saplings from the surrounding forest. One by one she plunged these into the ground in a circle and bent each one toward the center, where she entwined it with others to form the traditional beehive shape of the Mbuti hut. Then she weaved additional saplings horizontally and diagonally through the structure to the highest point, making a kind of geodesic dome with an entrance on one side through which I could crawl. The next step required the collecting of armfuls of mongongo leaves, which Sangali began to weave into the lattice of saplings from the ground up, each layer overlapping the one beneath it like tiles or shingles on a modern house. To provide greater strength, each leaf was pinned to the nearest sapling by its own stem.

By the time Sangali had a third of the required leaves in place on my new home the hunters and women were returning from the forest. They included people with names I would soon get to know such as Madada, Makubasi, Anjuway, Yauli, and Sefu, with their wives Miasa, Alondi, Sefini, Mukeyina, and Silina. At least two of the women carried baskets full of mushrooms, and the other women carried in their baskets the carcasses of five *mboloko* antelope killed at the net. Some of the hunters came and greeted me politely, one still holding his bloodied spear. Makubasi, who was a respected older hunter, presented me with the entire back leg of a red duiker, a medium-sized antelope. It was very generous of him, and also marked the acceptance of my presence by the community. When I asked if I could accompany them all on the next day's net hunt, they agreed. Makubasi had apparently been chosen by the band as *capita* to conform with the Bantu village system. As such he was a spokesman for the collective decisions and opinions of the band in dealing with the villagers but had no special authority or political power among the Mbuti themselves. As hunters and gatherers, the Mbuti are naturally acephalous—they do not have leaders or rulers, and decisions concerning the band are made by consensus.

Abruptly, lightning and thunder exploded from the black clouds that had drifted silently overhead. Quickly a friend rushed to help Sangali finish my hut, which was still only half covered with leaves. The rainstorm was almost upon us and it looked as if I would have to share someone else's hut after all, at least for the first night of my stay in Ekale. As it turned out, the hut to one side of mine was owned by Makubasi. The hut on the other side was occupied by two unmarried girls, named Makela and Kimbi. Each was a *museka,* the name given to girls who have reached puberty (and therefore sexual maturity) but are not yet married. They sat at a fire outside their hut, watching the progress of my new home with amused curiosity.

Because Makela was the daughter of Makubasi, he told both girls that they should give their hut to me and sleep outside by the fire that night. Both girls shyly smiled their agreement when I looked in their direction.

"What happens if it rains?" I asked with some embarrassment at my role of evictor.

"They'll find somewhere to sleep." Makubasi shrugged, concluding the conversation by disappearing into the hut he shared with his wife, Mukeyina.

At that moment a flash of lightning seemed to rip open the sky above us, and the rain started. I quickly threw my backpack in the girls' hut and stood for a moment in the rain, looking about me. Everybody was moving into the huts, where fires had been transferred in anticipation of the rain. I had already noticed that Abeli, Kachelewa, and Anziani had moved in with friends or relatives. The girls Makela and Kimbi had taken shelter in a nearby hut and were watching me smilingly from its doorway. Their hut stood invitingly before me, but it lacked its fire, which had been left outside and was quickly dying in the rain.

I ducked inside the girls' hut with feelings of guilt and gratitude. There had hardly been time to notice that Makela and Kimbi were both attractive young women whose cheerful goodwill reflected the pleasures of the present carefree and all too brief part of their lives when they could still enjoy the privileges of adulthood without its responsibilities. I hoped they would come by after the rain and light my fire. I could try to prove my bush lore by attempting to light it myself with rain-soaked materials. But an Mbuti would simply bring over some burning embers from another fire and effortlessly provide an instant flame. If I became lucky, the girls—or more likely one of their mothers—might even cook for me, a chore I could not do for myself without ridicule in a society where men, especially visitors, do not generally cook for themselves.

But what on earth was I doing anyway in the center of a soggy African rain forest? What had drawn me away from the comfort and security of my own world? What if I became too ill to walk out? Or what if I awakened the next morning to find myself all alone among a billion trees, hopelessly lost forever?

Here in the Ituri forest there was one compelling reason for my presence.

The African Pygmies have been irresistible to me since I first read about them as a student. But my curiosity and impatient nature would not allow me to accept only what I could find between the covers of a book. So I made a youthful decision that one day I had to see and hear and feel the reality of their lives for myself. My first visit to the Ituri was in 1954, while I was living and working in Kenya.

In the years between, I lived in several African countries and studied four African languages. Along the way, I had made 16 mm documentary films on such diverse subjects as African woodcarving art, the music of the Chopi people of Mozambique, and the hunting of elephants by a native African hunter in Zambia—about which I also wrote a book, *Black Elephant Hunter.*

Somehow I also managed to become a member of a museum expedition to northern Greenland, where I lived among a hunting group of polar Eskimos for two months and made a documentary film on those most northerly of all the world's peoples. The comparisons between these Arctic hunters and the equatorial Mbuti Pygmies have continued to interest me ever since. Amidst this activity, I also managed to spend nine months in India and Nepal, where I made a documentary film on the people of that vibrant subcontinent and another on the young Western travelers who wander with the seasons from the snowy Himalayas to Banares and the golden beaches of Goa.

However, my main interest and lifelong love affair has been with Africa and its wonderfully heterogeneous people. But how does one get around Africa without independent means? The down-to-earth answer was to find a job from time to time, preferably one in which I could apply myself as a social anthropologist, thereby furthering my knowledge of people, and of Africans in particular.

I twice worked on the remote Zaire border of Zambia for the Anglo-American (mining) Corporation for a total of eight years as a government-licensed African Personnel Officer. For the last three and a half years of that stint, I was also resident African Township Manager. The legal requirements for being granted a government license for this work included sitting for and passing the official written and oral civil service native language examinations, and I was the only European living among and responsible for 4,500 African migrant workers and their families from numerous tribes in Zambia and other countries, including Angola, Zaire, and Tanzania.

While I was with Anglo-American, I personally handled and settled at least 15,000 cases involving tribal disputes, domestic problems, and work-related incidents. During those final three and a half years in the Zambian forest, I was the only white resident in an all-African community, and there were often weeks at a time when I did not meet another white person. But although I loved the diverse tribal peoples I lived among, I never lost my fascination for the Mbuti Pygmies across the border in what was then the Congo, and is now Zaire.

As I worked those long hours, from time to time I would remind myself that out there, within a few days' drive on almost impassable roads, was a surviving group of true hunters and gatherers—a living example of how human society functioned before farming and pastoralism began to replace the nomadic ways of homo sapiens ten thousand years ago. I knew I would spend the rest of my life regretting it if I did not record everything I could about them on both film and paper before their ways disappeared entirely.

The Mbuti were not only still around, but they had unique qualities that made them different from all other peoples on earth. In blood grouping tests, according to Jean Hiernaux, director of research at the National Center for Scientific Research, Paris, the Mbuti show "ultra-African" frequencies in a number of genetic traits in the blood. "They stand at or near to the end of the African range of variation, at the opposite pole to the European or Arab values." Although there is no direct archaeological evidence (the Mbuti never did have a stone age, and it is doubtful if a fossil Pygmy will ever be found because of the nature of the soil in the damp forest), Hiernaux estimates that the Mbuti may have been living genetically separate in the forest for at least twenty thousand years. Taking all his findings together, it would seem that the Mbuti Pygmies may be among the most African of all Africa's surviving peoples. The Mbuti are different even to the tips of their fingers. The total ridge count of their fingerprints is the lowest ever found anywhere in the world.

Their best-known difference, of course, is their shortness. But while it is generally agreed that the Mbuti are the smallest people in the world (men average four feet eight and a half inches, women four feet six inches), nobody has yet provided an entirely satisfactory reason for their size. Many theories have been suggested: a scarcity of food, a genetic condition caused by inbreeding, natural selection and adaptation to the forest environment, a growth-hormone deficiency, to name a few. However, an article published in the *New England Journal of Medicine* (February 1982) indicates that although Pygmies resemble people with a growth-hormone deficiency, tests reveal normal levels of the hormone in their blood. Instead, these studies found Pygmies to have a major deficiency of a substance called IGF-1, one of a class of secondary growth factors which the researchers call "possibly the principal growth factor in human beings."

Paradoxically, we may now know why Pygmies are so short but not why they are deficient in IGF-1. Could their size have been caused by the continued weak levels of ultraviolet irradiation in the gloom of the forest? Or the high humidity? Or the forces of social rather than natural selection? Perhaps among the original and more localized "Pygmy" stock twenty thousand years ago, tall people became unfashionable—or even unpopular enough to be killed by a majority of shorter people.

While I was living in central Africa in 1959 and 1963, thousands of the tall Watutsi tribe were massacred by the Bahutu, a shorter tribe who lived among them. Such were the Bahutu's hatred and fear for the lanky Watutsi that they chopped off the legs of many of them so that they would be the same height as themselves.

The slaughter was the short people's way of rebelling against generations of the tall people's aristocratic rule. Both groups had lived peacefully together for four hundred years. But now, being short was "in" and being tall was dangerous to your health. Since the Bahutu formed 80 percent of the population, it's conceivable that if these massacres had occurred in earlier times, not one tall person, including those of mixed blood, would have been left alive to carry on their genetic line, and had this happened long ago, the story might have only survived as myth.

I do not suggest this as the most probable cause of the Pygmies' being so small. Rather, I present it as an unusual, documented case of how a known population experienced an abrupt loss of height-producing genes.

So much for reflection and why I was now crouched inside a flimsy Mbuti hut, watching raindrops splatter into the mud just an arm's length away.

Absently, I scooped out a channel in the mud to divert water from running into my hut and wondered if the rain would stop before everybody in the camp fell asleep. I was tired from my long walk into the heart of the forest, but I hoped not too tired to appreciate whatever social activity Ekale might develop on my first night there. But then, twenty-four hours more or less in the Ituri meant little to a society where birthdays and people's ages are unknown, where recorded time existed only in my mind, and a watch was an unnecessary, ostentatious trinket. To the Mbuti, an evening lost to the rain would inevitably be followed by a rainless one.

It had been a long day, and I lay down on the damp, rough

ground with my backpack as a pillow, listening to the rain beating loudly against the leaves of my fragile, biodegradable shelter. I moved to avoid a steady drip and reflected on my good fortune. I had arrived in Ekale tired and hungry, but with no more than a few scratches and a bruise to show for the walk back in time to the world of the Mbuti Pygmies. I looked through the entrance of my hut and in the fleeting twilight of dusk saw the ghostly shapes of the other huts standing in the rain. I wondered what earlier travelers to Africa had thought on meeting with these little people who reflect a way of life that human beings lived for tens of thousands of years before the advent of "civilization."

# 2

## Encounter With A Pharaoh

The earliest known record of the Pygmies' existence was written in about 2250 B.C. It was a letter from the Egyptian Pharaoh Nefrikare, Pepi II, in the Sixth Dynasty of the Old Kingdom. Addressed to his commander, Harkhuf, Governor of the South, it read:

> I have noted thy letter, which thou hast sent in order that the King might know thou hast descended in safety from Yam with the army which was with thee. Thou hast said in this thy letter that thou hast brought a dancing dwarf of the god from the land of spirits. . . .
>
> Come northward to the court immediately; thou shalt bring this dwarf with thee, which thou bringest living and healthy from the land of spirits, for the dances of the god, to gladden the heart of the King of Upper and Lower Egypt, Neferkere, who lives forever. When he goes down with thee into the vessel, appoint excellent people, who shall be beside him on each side of the vessel; take care lest he fall into the water. When he sleeps at night appoint excellent people, who shall sleep beside him in his tent. My majesty desires to see this dwarf more than the gifts of Sinai and Punt.
>
> Breasted's *Ancient Records of Egypt*

Thus, to the god-king Nefrikare, a dancing Pygmy was more desirable than anything else Harkhuf might bring back from the exotic forests of the South.

Many signs of the Egyptians' fascination with Pygmies survived down through the centuries. The name given to the figure of a Pygmy on a monument of the old empire has been deciphered as Akka, a name by which some Mbuti are known today. And today, nearly a thousand miles to the west, in the Central African Republic, there is also a group of Pygmies known as Aka.

Bes, the god of Egyptian folk tradition, patron of music and dancing and of children, first appeared c. 2000 B.C. on ointment jars, mirrors, and other articles apparently inspired by Pygmies brought for entertainment from the source lands of the Nile. Ivory statuettes found in a tomb of the Twelfth Dynasty portray naked Pygmies dancing, an activity for which they may have been most valued. Dated c. 1950 B.C., these statuettes possess both an extraordinary realism and a close anthropometric resemblance to "modern" Pygmies.

It is apparent from Pharaoh Nefrikare's letter and other factors that Pygmies from tropical Africa were known in Egypt in 2250 B.C., and for hundreds of years thereafter. While minimal ethnological information is provided from this source, the record at least indicates that the Pygmies' love of dance was no less then than it is now, more than 4,000 years later.

More than a thousand years later, the Greek poet Homer mentions the Pygmies in his *Iliad:*

> So when inclement winters vex the plain
> With piercing frosts, or thick descending rain,
> To warmer seas the cranes embodied fly,
> With noise and order, through the midway sky;
> To Pygmy nations wounds and death they bring,
> And all the war descends upon the wing.
> *Iliad,* III, 6–10, Alexander Pope translation

No one knows why Homer—even assuming it was a case of poetic license—had hostile cranes flying off to battle with the little Pygmies. Nor does he tell us what happened when they reached their destination. Perhaps there's a lost verse somewhere describing squadrons of dead cranes with poisoned arrows protruding from their blood-stained plumage.

The next historical mention of the Pygmies comes some hundreds of years later from another Greek, the historian Herodotus. He wrote of a group of Nasamonians who traveled south across the desert to a region of trees, where they were captured by Pygmies whose language they could not understand.

Aristotle, in his *History of Animals,* mentions Pygmies in his description of storks or cranes. He said the cranes fly to the lakes above Egypt from which flows the Nile. "There dwell the Pygmies, and this is no fable," he emphasized, apparently anticipating disbelief in the existence of the little people. Does this famous philosopher mention Pygmies and cranes together just because Homer had? And did Homer's reference to cranes stem from the early Egyptians' symbolism of these birds battling the falling waters of the Nile? Or were the cranes actually the man-sized ostrich still found in the Sudan today? We'll probably never know.

However, we do know that it was the Greeks who were responsible for the name *Pygmy,* deriving the word from a unit of measure denoting the distance between a man's elbow and his knuckles. (If the height of giants was often exaggerated, the shortness of Pygmies was too.)

By the first century B.C., traders from Arabia had established colonies on tropical Africa's east coast. They were visited over the centuries by Indians, Persians, Indonesians, Malayans, and Chinese who came to trade goods that included ivory, gold, tortoiseshell, copper, iron, and rhinoceros horn. In time, slaves became an important export for the Arabs, who as traders would survive the advent of the Portuguese and other European colonizers. Adventurously, the Arabs regularly penetrated the interior of equatorial Africa, reaching, among other places, the country today known as Zaire. Few records exist, but one Abed bin Juma told of meeting some members of a mysterious race of dwarfs whose existence had long been regarded as a fable. These dwarfs said that in their country there were boundless treasures of ivory. They themselves attached no value to it, and even wondered why foreigners wanted it, as it was no good to eat. Enticed further by these fabulous narratives, Abed bin Juma's caravan, after six more days' march, reached the land of the dwarfs "but was very fiercely received by the malicious little demons who sprang from the soil around like mushrooms, and showered their poisoned arrows on the travellers, causing them endless losses. Only thirty were able to escape with bare life."

It is of interest to mention the Alur of today's Uganda and their tradition of Pygmies, near whom they once apparently lived. Although no longer aware of their present existence or location, according to anthropologist Aidan Southall the Alur remember them

as of dwarf stature, yet of great ferocity and cunning, and as skillful hunters, especially of elephants. The Alur called them "Jupunenakane?" (The People of Where-did-you-see-me?) because when you met a Pygmy he always asked you where you had seen him coming. If you said you had only just seen him he would attack you at once for thus slighting his stature, so you pointed to a distant hill and affirmed that you had seen him right over there, and all was well and friendly.

Similar stories have been reported from as far away as northeastern and southern Tanzania and among the Lunda of Zambia regarding a pre-Bantu, bushmanlike stock long since vanished from the areas concerned, indicating that people of small stature may have been sensitive about their shortness since prehistoric times.

In 1699 Edward Tyson, M.D., Fellow of the Royal College of Physicians in England, wrote a book entitled *Anatomy of a Pygmy Compared with That of a Monkey, an Ape and a Man,* in which he proceeded to demonstrate that "Pygmies are either apes or monkeys, and not men. . . ." It is now known that the skeletons he obtained from Africa, and on which he based his studies, were of chimpanzees.

Early European explorers passed along—and possibly distorted or misinterpreted—stories they heard about the legendary Pygmies from non-Pygmy Negro tribes, including one tale (as told to the early explorer Dapper by the Yaga tribe) explaining the little people's success at collecting ivory. The Pygmies, so the story went, "have the power of making themselves invisible and consequently can slay an elephant with little trouble." French explorer de Lauture was told of a dwarf people who had tails. And so the simple fact of their existence in ancient Egyptian times had degenerated over the centuries into apparent myth.

It was a French-American explorer, Paul du Chaillu, who in the nineteenth century again verified the existence of the Pygmies and reestablished them as human. In his 1867 book, *A Journey to Ashango-Land,* he describes his first encounter with them— a band in the depths of Gabon's rain forest who he said were called the "Obongos, or dwarfed wild negroes." His detailed account of their appearance (including height measurements averaging well under five feet), their way of life, and their relationship to the local villagers leaves no doubt about the authenticity of this historical meeting.

> The Obongos [he said] never remain long in one place. They are eminently a migratory people, moving from place to place whenever game becomes scarce. But they do not wander very far; that is, the Obongos who live within the territory of the Ashango Negroes do not go out of that territory—they are called the Obongos of the Ashangos. Those who live among the Njavi negroes are called Obongo-Njavi—and the same with other tribes.

At the end of his visit, his Ashango guides informed him that if he wanted to buy an Obongo, they would be happy to catch him one.

The next best known documented meeting between European and Pygmy occurred when the German scientist-explorer Georg

Schweinfurth reached the court of the Negro king Munza of the Monbutto. In his book *Heart of Africa,* published in 1874, Schweinfurth describes his excitement at meeting his first Pygmy, a man named Adimokoo. He then goes on to tell of the king offering him male and female slaves in exchange for two dogs he had brought with him. Schweinfurth wrote that he refused the Negro slaves, but did except a fifteen-year-old Akka Pygmy youth named Nsewuc in exchange for one of his dogs. He made the young man his *protégé* and shared his meals and travels with him for ten months until Nsewue died of dysentery in Berber, still technically a slave.

Sir Henry Morton Stanley reached the Ituri forest in 1887 and in his book *In Darkest Africa* he recorded this first meeting with a Pygmy:

At this settlement I saw the first specimen of the tribe of dwarfs who were said to be thickly scattered north of the Ituri [river], from the Ngaiyu eastward. She measured thirty-three inches in height, and was a perfectly formed young woman of about seventeen, of a glistening and smooth sleekness of body. Her figure was that of a miniature coloured lady, not wanting in a certain grace, and her face was very prepossessing. Her complexion was that of a quadroon [a person who is one-fourth Negro], or of the colour of yellow ivory. Her eyes were magnificent, but absurdly large for such a small creature—almost as large as that of a young gazelle; full, protruding, and extremely lustrous. Absolutely nude, the little demoiselle was quite possessed, as though she was accustomed to be admired, and really enjoyed inspection.

Later he reports that his men "made a splendid capture of Pygmies," four women and a boy. He singled out one of these women as being of the Akka group and described her "as being fitly characteristic of the link long sought between the average modern humanity and its Darwinian progenitors, and certainly deserving of being classed as an extremely low, degraded, almost a bestial type of human being." This indulgence of his imagination was followed by a kinder opinion of one of the other "Wambutti" women, which included the fact that she had perfect proportions, yet was only four feet four inches tall. By comparing her side by side with a local Bantu village woman and some of his men, he concluded "that these small creatures were a distinct race." Six months later he met his first Pygmy man, whom he regarded as "more venerable than the Menonium of Thebes. That little body," he wrote, "represents the oldest type of primeval man, descended from the outcasts of the earliest ages." Stanley measured the height of only four adult Pygmies, one woman of thirty-three inches, and two others fifty-two inches each. The man mentioned here was recorded as forty-eight inches high and described by Stanley as having the dignity of Adam. The "little maid" with him—who was nude—"had the womanliness of a miniature Eve." Later Stanley states that the Wambutti vary in height from three feet to four feet six inches.

In his quest to rescue Emin Pasha, Stanley crossed the then unknown Ituri forest twice, losing many men to sickness and hostile non-Pygmy tribes. He specifically mentions being guided by Pygmies on this difficult journey. Of the Pygmies' value as allies and of their ability to fight, he wrote, "When arrows are arrayed against arrows, poison against poison, and craft against craft, probably the party assisted by the Pygmies would prevail. Their diminutive size, superior woodcraft, greater malice, would make formidable opponents." It seemed that the great explorer continued to have mixed feelings about Pygmies, but when he later discusses the near starvation his expedition suffered in the Ituri, he gives credit to the Pygmies for teaching his relatively helpless and starving expedition of "modern" men how to survive in the wilderness by gathering and preparing a wild bean that "sustained them through so many days of awful famine."

The expedition's officers took at least two Mbuti Pygmies with them as personal servants on leaving the Ituri, a "young damsel" and an apparently unrelated young man. Months later they had so impressed Stanley that he wrote, "The Pygmies showed by their conduct that they were related to all that was best and noble in human nature." He does not explain what conduct caused this lavish praise, if praise it was. It is possible that he was thinking of the Mbuti as noble savages.

Ituri Forest, Zaire.

Mbuti hunting camp.

Mbuti family.

Children playing.

Women with child preparing food at hut.

Girls carrying firewood.

Drinking from forest stream with leaf as cup.

Girl with basket.

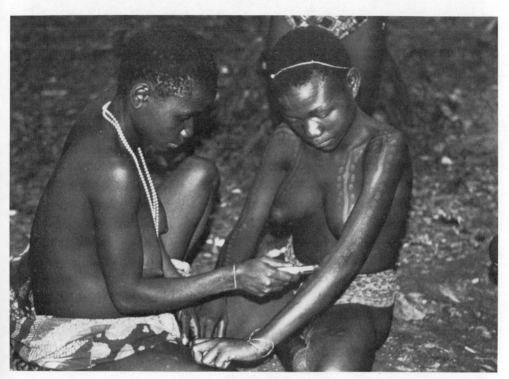

Woman paints friend with lipstick
given by author.

Making bark cloth using elephant tusk hammer.

What the Mbuti thought of the white men is not recorded. Nor does Stanley's book tell us if these Mbuti "servants" had been captured like the others. The young damsel taken from the Ituri by Stanley became ill after a year with the expedition and was abandoned along the way. Details of her incapacity and of where she was abandoned were not provided. It would be reasonable to assume that if she was left with other human beings, such a people would have had little sympathy for her, being almost certainly of a different language and culture.

It is perhaps of interest to reprint here the prices, in "sheeting cloths," of slaves in 1876 at the market in Ujiji (where Stanley earlier met Livingstone) as published by Stanley in his book *Through the Dark Continent*. It could be assumed that the young damsel and the young man taken by Stanley and his men to accompany them were in the most highly prized age bracket of 13–18. Without further research, one may only speculate on why pubescent and teenage girls were valued so highly over all other categories of slaves.

|  |  |  |  |  |  |  | Sheeting cloths of 4 yards long |
|---|---|---|---|---|---|---|---|
| 1 slave boy between | 10 | and | 13 | years old | | | 16 |
| 1 slave girl | " | 10 | " | 13 | " | " | 50 to 80 |
| 1 " " | " | 13 | " | 18 | " | " | 80 to 200 |
| 1 slave woman | " | 18 | " | 30 | " | " | 80 to 130 |
| 1 " " | " | 30 | " | 50 | " | " | 10 to 40 |
| 1 " boy | " | 13 | " | 18 | " | " | 16 to 50 |
| 1 " man | " | 18 | " | 50 | " | " | 10 to 50 |

To this market, according to Stanley, slaves were sent by the Wajiji and Wangwana tribes and by the Arabs. The currency often used was cloth from Massachusetts and Manchester.

A. J. Mounteney-Jephson was one of Stanley's officers, and he wrote a book about the expedition in which he occasionally takes time to describe the Pygmies (*Emin Pasha and the Rebellion at the Equator*, 1980). His style is more objective, and certainly more to the point, than that of Stanley himself. I quote a few passages taken from various pages of the book written by this nineteenth-century eyewitness about the Pygmies he met.

They are of a light brown reddish colour, and are sometimes of a yellowish hue. Most of them are from 4 feet to 4 feet 1 inch in height. . . . Ornaments and tribal marks are not usually seen among them, nor do they mutilate themselves in any way. In the forests the men and children are always absolutely naked, the women wear fringes of green leaves around their waists, and occasionally small strips of skin or bark cloth. . . . From an anthropological point of view the dwarfs are by no means a degenerate race, as some writers have pretended. . . . After settling in some place where game abounds, they begin hunting, and, out of the produce, exchange feathers, skins, meat, ivory, etc., with the villagers, who, in return, give them such foods as they require. As long as this system is fairly observed, they are on good terms with the villagers, but if they consider themselves slighted in the smallest degree—and they are very ready to take offence—they do not hesitate to retaliate on the villagers, laying ambuscades for them, shooting at them from behind trees, killing them, and pillaging their fields and banana plantations. They are excellent shots, and are very revengeful, their tiny bows and arrows being most deadly weapons; so it may be easily understood that the natives are always anxious to be on good terms with them, and seldom willingly molest them. They often stay for some time in one place, if game is plentiful, and the villagers friendly, and only leave it when the game becomes scarce. The dwarfs do not carry any household goods, cooking pots, etc., on their peregrinations, and usually cook their food wrapped in leaves and placed on the red-hot embers. They occasionally, however, get cooking pots from the village near which they are camping. They are, in fact, as primitive as it is possible for a people to be. . . . The Pygmies generally settle down near some small brook in the midst of the forest, and erect small huts for the married people, boys and girls merely making themselves small shelters by bending down small saplings and covering them with leaves. The huts are very small, being about four feet in height and a beehive shape; long thin sticks are made into a rough framework, and covered with green leaves. . . . It is evident

that agriculture is not practiced by them. . . . They are very reticent and reserved, but it seems they have a language of their
own in their permanent settlements, though in an ordinary way,
they speak the language of the country in which they are staying. . . . Many of the women are good-looking and well formed,
and the neighbouring tribes willingly take them for wives when
they can. . . . The men make fair servants, but will not do hard
work like the women, and are always restless. Both men and
women, however young they were brought to the station, always
preserved some independence of spirit, which made them at times
rather obstinate. . . . The dwarfs we had with us never did well
in the open country, they did not seem able to stand the sun and
cold nights, and were constantly ill with fever.

A trans-African expedition on foot in the last century is not
the ideal occasion on which to study an elusive, nomadic people
called Wambutti by Stanley. Numerous languages must have
been encountered on the journey. Dozens of men died along the
way. For the survivors each day might have been their last. For
Mounteney-Jephson to gather the information he did on the
Mbuti was extraordinary. This Victorian gentleman does not
say so, or might have been unaware of it, but the "occasional"
use of strips of (animal) skin or tree bark may well have indicated
menstruating women.

While it is of passing sociological interest that a young man
so far from home should have described Mbuti women as "good-
looking and well formed," Mounteney-Jephson's chance obser-
vation on the Mbuti's linguistic ability may be ultimately more
important to the study of African languages. "It seems," he
wrote, "they have a language of their own in their permanent
settlements, though in an ordinary way, they speak the language
of the country in which they are staying."

"Permanent settlements" here can mean the Mbuti's nomadic
hunting camps in the deep forest away from the villages of the
agriculturalists, as opposed to the camps they periodically make
near the village or villages with which they have chosen to
associate. If, with the use of interpreters, Mounteney-Jephson
verified that the Mbuti he met spoke a language different from

that of any villager, he may well have been listening to the original Mbuti language now apparently lost forever (although Austrian anthropologist and missionary Reverend Paul Schebesta would later suggest that the Lese language spoken by the Ituri Sudanic cultivators of the same name may be the original Mbuti language).

When the height of some hundreds of male and female Mbuti was recently measured it was found that the males averaged four feet eight and a half inches and the females four feet six inches. If Mounteney-Jephson's figure of forty-eight and a half inches for the average height of an Mbuti can be accepted, it would seem that they have increased their stature by more than six inches in the past hundred years. This could possibly be attributed to the diet of cultivated foods they obtain from their agricultural neighbors, increasingly varied in this century. Intermarriage with the taller villagers may not have been the dominant factor here, as I shall explain later.

Assuming that Stanley had an accurate measuring device (whatever it was) and did not exaggerate, the "little demoiselle" he admired was, at thirty-three inches tall, a remarkably small person.

It was not until 1929 that a comprehensive study of all the Mbuti groups in the Ituri was commenced by the Reverend Paul Schebesta. Much of the multivolumed published results of his ambitious studies, especially as they define the Ituri's various Negro and Mbuti groups and their languages, remain valid today. Schebesta was probably the first outsider to call the Mbuti "children" when he referred to them as "children of the wild" and "children of nature." In recording their folklore, he wrote that the Mbuti saw themselves as the "children of God." Schebesta himself in time became known in the Ituri as "the father of the Bambuti." Like Stanley before him, he was impressed by the diminutiveness of some of the Mbuti he met. "In this camp, too," he wrote in *Among Congo Pigmies,* "I saw the smallest Pigmy I had ever encountered. It sounds almost incredible that a fully grown and normally developed woman with a healthy six-year-old child, could be only three feet eleven and a half inches in height."

An American anthropologist, Patrick Putnam, was among the next on the scene to study the Mbuti. He would live in the Ituri almost continuously for about twenty years until his premature death from a tropical illness in the forest in 1953. He established a permanent base on the edge of the road where it crosses the Epulu River, a place that for decades would be on the map as Camp Putnam. Today there is little sign of the large mud-walled guest house and hospital that Putnam built, a place that became a sort of mecca for visitors to the Ituri, and where he would entertain guests by having the local band of Mbuti perform their famous dances.

One of the next important anthropologists in the history of the Mbuti was a young Englishman, Colin Turnbull, who knew and stayed with Patrick Putnam before he died and who would eventually write *The Forest People* (1961) and *Wayward Servants* (1965). Unlike Schebesta, Turnbull decided to concentrate his main studies on a single Mbuti band. He did this for one calendar year and chose as his subject the same band that had been associated with Patrick Putnam for about a generation.

It was, incidentally, among the survivors, relatives, and immediate descendants of this same band that I was now camping on a brief visit. I was just a six-hour walk away from Camp Putnam, now known as Epulu. Other anthropologists, including Schebesta, would claim that this band was particularly acculturated and not representative of other net hunting bands, much less all Mbuti hunters and gatherers.

However, it is a fact that all Mbuti have been acculturated by the villagers for hundreds of years and, to some extent, by government administrators and missionaries for generations. To recreate a pure Mbuti culture, it would be necessary to remove all traces of Negro influence—whatever they all are—including presumably most if not all of the languages the Mbuti now speak.

Meanwhile, the Mbuti's own hunting-and-gathering culture has remained remarkably intact because they have learned to adjust their nomadic lives to the two worlds they live in, the world of the forest and the outside world of the villagers. Rather than losing a culture, the various Mbuti groups have adopted parts of the cultures of the villagers while retaining most of their own. It is their way of getting the best of both worlds, and this basic relationship has not changed since prehistoric times. An Mbuti hunting band today still leads much the same life and has much the same village relationships as forest Pygmies described by du Chaillu and Mounteney-Jephson more than a century ago.

# 3

## Hunting, Gathering, and The Molimo

A bubbling sound awakened me in the darkness just before dawn. I reached out and felt the sticks and leaves of my shelter, reassured that it was not a dream. I really was lying in an Mbuti hut in the center of a primeval African forest. Abruptly, the bubbling was interrupted by a hacking cough, and I knew then that somebody with a water pipe was having an early morning smoke of bangi in the hut next to mine. Leafy walls do little to impede sounds between huts in a camp of nomadic Mbuti Pygmies, especially during the still hours between dusk and dawn.

I rolled over on the rough, earthen floor and peered out the open doorway at the dim shapes of the other huts. The bubbling noise had stopped, and from another direction an infant began to cry and was soon soothed by an attentive mother. From another hut came the first sounds of conversation, a man and woman talking, their every word carrying clearly into the neighboring huts. That seemed to be the signal for the camp to wake up. The light was stronger now, and one by one people wandered out of their huts and began their day in much the same way their ancestors—and mine—had for thousands of years. There were neighbors to greet, infants to wash, food to prepare, plans to discuss. I felt that I shared their humanity and was a part of it, for their world was fundamentally my world too.

But here there would be no children to get ready for school, no rush-hour traffic to fight, no bus, train, or airplane to catch, no time clock to punch. For these nomadic Mbuti Pygmies, this would be just another day without name, number, or written record. In the daily quest for food, it would be remembered only as long as events made it memorable.

It takes little to create a cheerful mood in an Mbuti camp, only a dry, friendly forest and signs that the hunting is good—everything that a reasonable person could ask for. Children squealed and laughed as they chased each other around the huts. A group of larger boys and girls were taking turns swinging on a vine that hung from a tall tree. A young mother sang a gentle lullaby to her infant while her friends prepared foods, tended other small children, and brought smoldering logs outside from their huts to start fires for cooking.

It was the kind of morning the Mbuti like, with sunlight streaming through the trees above and no rain on the way. Soon the clinging moisture of the night would be gone, again leaving the forest a fit place in which to hunt and gather food. It was a happy camp, but only the women and children readily showed it with their bright mood and enthusiasm. The men and grown boys remained mostly reserved and aloof from the early morning activities of the women and girls. Only when the food was ready would they mingle again.

I followed a line of chatting women and girls leaving camp to fetch water. They laughed playfully when I joined them on a path through the trees, for usually men and women do not go to the river together. Yet as the Mbuti do not wash or bathe every day, the women were my surest way of finding the river. (Mbuti camps are usually built away from rivers and streams to avoid mosquitoes.) The older men were sitting at the communal fire sharing a pipe of bangi. The young married hunters sat separately, passing around their own pipe of bangi, while the young bachelors stood talking in a group just outside the camp, glancing from time to time at the unmarried girls.

The women led me to a stream flowing gently beneath a vaulted archway of moss-covered trees, its clear water bubbling invitingly beneath a little waterfall. I wandered upstream alone and soon found a secluded spot for bathing. The deepest part only reached my knees, but it was refreshing to wash off the mud and sweat from the previous day's march. From downstream I could hear much laughing and splashing, and I wondered for how many thousands of years the forest had echoed with these delightful sounds. A movement caught my eye and I looked up at the bank to see two boys staring at me curiously. From then on, there would be no doubt in their minds; I was white all over, not just on my hands and face. I smiled and invited them into the water. They called into the trees behind them, and three other boys of various ages joined them in jumping into the stream beside me. I splashed water at them and they splashed back and at each other. They thought the entire affair hilarious, especially when my shoes and clothes were knocked off a rock into the water and I grimaced in mock disgust as I held them up, dripping wet.

Back at the camp, I watched the women prepare the morning meal, each in her own way. A woman peeled some bananas and neatly put the skins in a pile. Another woman carelessly flung plantain skins over her shoulder to land somewhere behind her hut. She then placed the newly skinned fruit directly on the fire to cook. One woman was peeling a cassava root, its wet pulp gleaming whitely in the shade of the trees. It was obvious that these Mbuti net hunters and their wives were efficient enough with their net hunting to produce more meat than they required for their own needs, for it was from the trading of such excess meat that they had acquired the cassava, bananas, and other cultivated foods from the villagers. Of the items that do not grow naturally in the forest, the ones the Mbuti like most are the banana and its coarser cousin, the plantain. Many an antelope has died in exchange for a bunch of bananas.

I was looking over my almost completed hut when Abeli came by, carrying an empty cooking pot. "Rice?" he asked. "Do you want some rice cooked?" I nodded and we crawled into the hut where I had slept the night before, a place that sheltered all my worldly goods of the moment. I handed Abeli a beer bottle filled with palm oil and corked with a rolled-up leaf and then gave him the bag of precious rice (precious because there was no place where I could purchase more when it ran out). I watched as he poured enough rice into the pot for about ten people.

"Is that for you, Kachelewa, Anziani, and myself?" I inquired.

"Yes." He shrugged as he went off to have the rice washed and cooked by Sangali and Anziani. Abeli was not one for unnecessary explanations, but I was glad that the rice and any other foods I gave him would apparently be shared among his relatives and friends, for I wanted to show my gratitude to these people who were allowing me to become a part of their daily lives.

Abeli was a serious young Mbuti caught between the worlds of the forest and the village. He liked to stay at Epulu and had somehow acquired a tattered shirt and short trousers. Yet his immediate relatives spent many months every year roaming the forest, the place where he was born and reared and that provided the meat that probably paid for his clothes. As an Mbuti, he could survive in the forest without the village, but not in the village without the forest. Only when he imitated the villagers and cultivated his own food would he be independent of the forest—and the villagers.

On a tree stump near me, a youth sat, lengthening his father's hunting net by weaving in twine newly made from the kusa vine. The finished mesh was remarkably symmetrical and could well have been factory made. Altogether I counted about nine hunting nets about the camp, some of them neatly coiled and ready to be carried on a hunter's shoulder into the forest. Three of them were being repaired by hunters. Although both men and women may gather the bark of the kusa vine and roll it into twine, it is the man's task to weave the net and repair it when necessary, just as only he may make arrows or put a new string on a bow, or work on anything else that has to do with the tools of the hunter. In the same way, only women weave the baskets traditionally used by them to gather and carry food. The other main items of value in an Mbuti camp—cooking pots and metal knives—are acquired ready-made from the villagers, for the Mbuti have never learned to work with clay, stone, or iron.

From experience, I had brought a bag of salt into the forest, and it wasn't long before every family in the camp had come to me for a handful of this popular item. Like the rice, it would be used up all too soon. The Mbuti share their food willingly enough with other members of the band, and I believe that this generosity would have extended to me for a time if I had arrived in their camp without food, or without anything to offer in exchange for food. In the same way, they hoped that the foods I brought into the forest would be shared around, and not just among those who came with me as guides. So now the bag of rice that would have lasted me a month might be used up in a couple of days. This is one reason I have sometimes found myself sooner than expected eating an all-Mbuti diet, which may include such tasty items as elephant, pig, pangolin, monkey, rat, snake, grubs, termites, and several varieties of mushrooms, fruits, nuts, mbau seeds, roots, and vegetables, all of which exist wild in the forest for those skillful enough to find them.

When the inevitable time came that I ran out of my own food, I would offer either goods or money in exchange for Mbuti fare. The goods I carried on this occasion included pocket knives, magnifying glasses (my idea of waterproof fire makers), nylon fishing line, and hooks. From time to time I would give money and empty containers, plastic bags, and the like to someone walking to the road. With luck they would bring back rice, oil, salt, bananas, and other items to eat with the venison or whatever meat was in camp, if any. The price I paid for this service included giving away more than half of the food soon after it arrived in the camp.

The road has been cut through the forest long enough for the Mbuti to know what paper money is, but not every Mbuti knows how to count into the higher numbers or to judge the real value of money. To enhance my acceptability as a guest of the community, I also brought two cartons of cigarettes, for I have yet to meet an Mbuti who does not smoke. Because they cannot afford to buy cigarettes from a roadside store, they usually smoke dried tobacco leaves acquired from the villagers who grow them. They smoke this in their pipes, sometimes mixing it with bangi. When I was present they learned to ask me for pieces of paper in which to roll the tobacco into cigarettes.

Soon everybody had settled down for breakfast. Among the foods I saw at the various family groups were boiled bananas, roasted plantains, cassava, stewed leafy vegetables gathered wild from the forest, and meat—altogether a better selection than usual for breakfast in an Mbuti camp. The cassava had been pounded into a coarse flour in the traditional way and boiled with very little water, creating a thick, puttylike substance to be eaten by hand. I took a plate from my pack and joined Abeli's group around their fire, where I was given a piece of the aging antelope leg presented to me by Makubasi the previous day and which I had passed on to Abeli, hoping never to see it again. The bottle of village-produced palm oil I had brought would be used to make it and the other food more palatable to us all.

We shared common dishes, each person taking a handful of cassava in turn, shaping it in one hand, and dipping it into the vegetables and juices. I had the only plate but ate with my fingers like the others. As guests, Abeli and I were privileged to have the only chairs, which had been simply made by lashing three sticks together in the middle with a piece of vine and spreading them into a kind of three-legged stool. There was no cushion or padding of any kind. One just somehow sat wedged between the three upright sticks. The others sat on logs or on little pieces of wood on the ground.

The meal was eaten in an agreeable, leisurely fashion. The plantains and meat were politely passed around so that everybody received a fair share. At first nobody reached for the biggest or best parts or gulped their food down. Instead, each person savored what he or she ate as if it were a new and exotic dish. Nearby, Makela and Kimbi were eating with another girl of about the same age. From time to time all three of them smiled in our direction. Abeli and Kachelewa returned their glances readily enough, but did not smile back.

I politely refused more of the antelope leg now offered by Sangali's husband and instead took a piece of banana. I had lived in Africa long enough to have contracted and thankfully recovered from several of the more serious diseases endemic to the area. After such hard-won experience, I no longer felt it necessary to prove I could eat anything that came my way.

When we had all finished, Sangali wrapped some of the cassava and meat in mongongo leaves and gave the food to her eldest child, a boy of about eleven. As an apprentice hunter, he would carry it into the forest for his father, where it would be eaten as a midday meal. Most boys and youths were supposed to stay with their fathers or perhaps an uncle during the hunt. In this way they learned by example and were also useful as an extra pair of hands at otherwise unguarded sections of net.

About two hours after sunrise the hunters began to walk into the forest. They went in small groups or one by one, some carrying nets over their shoulders. Several men carried spears, and one or two had a bow and some arrows. Contact was maintained with those ahead by shouting and listening for the call that came back. The sound was uniquely Pygmy and was the same as that I had heard from Pygmies a thousand miles to the west—a series of loud "ooohs" that cheerfully echoed back and forth through the forest. The sound effectively transformed an awesome wilderness into a friendly place for a little band of humans who needed each other to survive.

I accompanied Kachelewa and Abeli to the *kungya,* a fire made in the forest some distance from the camp each morning before the hunt. Besides serving as a gathering place, its purpose was to honor the forest and to ask for its blessing on the hunt. The fire had been made earlier by one of the hunters while the others were having breakfast. Now all the hunters sat near this fire, some of them talking, others silent.

While they waited for the women to arrive, they burned small, fresh branches with green leaves still attached. From the burned ends of such sticks, they blackened parts of their faces, especially around the eyes. In this way, they wore a part of the hunting fire, which in turn had been made from the sacred forest, in order to bring good luck in the hunt. Painting this essence of the forest around their eyes was meant to magically help the hunters see the animals better.

The women began to arrive and wait nearby, most of them carrying large baskets in which they would collect mushrooms and other wild edibles along the way. If the hunt went well, these baskets would also be used to carry back any small antelope killed at the net. Back at the camp there remained a few people old enough to have grown sons to do their hunting for them. They would look after the children who were too young— or not young enough—to go on the hunt. Only children older than about ten and infants not yet weaned went on the hunt. Such an infant was slung from its mother's shoulder in a piece of animal skin and could be breast-fed even while its mother moved through the forest with the band of hunters.

Only when everybody had collected in the vicinity of the kungya did we all depart for the first place in the forest where the nets would be set up. From now on there was no shouting, and talking was done in whispers or not at all. Abeli had discarded his shirt and trousers and wore only the traditional Mbuti bark cloth. He seemed extraordinarily happy and grinned broadly when he said that he was not going to stay with me, but would join the hunters ahead. Young and eager, he had lost the somber mask he had seemed to adopt in the world of the village. Here in the forest, showing one's emotions was natural, desirable, and expected. Abeli had grown up in the forest an Mbuti, yet was just as thrilled with the hunt as I was. In moments he had disappeared with his peers among the trees, leaving me with the less energetic Kachelewa, whose name meant "late" or "to be late" in at least two of the African languages I know.

The first area chosen to place the nets was about a mile from the camp and contained the sort of vegetation where some nocturnal antelopes like to hide during the day. Working quietly, the hunters uncoiled their nets and attached them end to end in a half-circle about three hundred yards in diameter. Made from natural materials and suspended or tied from bushes or trees, the thin strands of the net formed an almost invisible barrier among the shadows. It was only three and a half feet high, however, and was meant mainly for the smaller kinds of forest antelope and was generally useless against full-grown specimens of such animals as the giant forest hog, the forest buffalo, the bongo antelope, and the okapi.

The forest was almost silent now except for a shrill symphony of crickets. The only people Kachelewa and I could see were Usaute and his young son, who continued to adjust their net here and there so that a tiny antelope wouldn't be able to nudge beneath it and escape. All I had to do was wait, an easy task.

The notion of man as hunter and chief provider is nowhere better exposed as a myth than in Mbuti net hunting.

In their traditional role as beaters, it is the women who must outwit the animals being hunted. They do this with stealth as they first silently approach the animals hidden among the trees, then with noise as they drive the animals into the net. A faulty sense of direction or poor timing by the women and the animals could well escape before the women can close the trap.

In contrast, it takes no particular skill to wait at the net or to kill an animal that runs blindly into it and becomes entangled in its mesh. Sometimes a woman will help guard the section of net owned by her husband. She may do this because she is an older woman and chooses this less strenuous work, or because her husband has no close relatives available to help him with his section of the net. More than any other people I know in Africa, the Mbuti are willing to ignore traditional male and female roles when total coordination is required to obtain food.

I knew that by now the women were probably in a position from which they would begin their advance into the half-circle of nets, driving any hiding animals ahead of them toward the waiting hunters. I wondered what would happen if they surprised a buffalo or leopard.

Just then the unseen women started to shout and beat the bushes as they began their drive. Careful not to move, I strained to see any animal that might come bounding toward me. To the left, I heard the terrified squealing of an mboloko, the local name for the little blue duiker antelope. A sudden silence meant it had perhaps died when a spear found its mark, or else it had escaped from the net. But within moments the first drive was over, and it turned out that the mboloko I heard was the only animal killed.

We quietly walked another mile and the nets were set up once more. This time I found myself waiting expectantly with Anjuway and his wife, Sefini, who guarded their net together. For the moment, Kachelewa had apparently taken his position somewhere else.

Anjuway ran a finger over the sharp edge of his rusted iron spear and muttered something about having nobody to help him except a woman and a Muzungu (in many African languages the word for a European or fair-skinned person of any origin except an African albino).

Again the distant women began to chant and shout as they advanced into the circle of waiting nets. Beside me, Anjuway stood poised with his spear; he was almost invisible in the shadows. Unarmed, his wife stood apart at another section of the net, ready to tackle whatever might dash toward us.

Suddenly two mboloko came running out of the shadows directly into the net between us. Anjuway stabbed the one nearest him with his spear, narrowly missing Sefini, who was gamely trying to grab the other one, a male with sharp little horns. She finally gripped it by the hind legs as it thrashed in the net, and lifted it off the ground as it squealed pathetically. Quickly, Anjuway slit its throat, using the blade of his spear as a knife. Sefini put both mboloko in her basket, a total weight of about fifty pounds, and began to help Anjuway roll up his net for the next drive. It was all quite efficient. Incidentally, among the various duiker antelopes, and including the okapi, of the Ituri forest, the females are larger than the males of their species, an interesting development for which I do not have an explanation.

In the next hunt, I joined the women beaters instead of waiting at the net. A young married woman named Miasa agreed to be my guide on this adventure. Both she and her friends thought it was an amusing idea to have me along, although there were two women who apparently thought I would scare the animals away.

Miasa was a cheerful, buxom young woman who was clearly popular among her peers. She seemed tireless in everything she did. During the walk to the next net-hunt location, I was fascinated to see her skill in gathering wild edible things along the way. In the dark shadows beneath a dense cover of foliage, she somehow spotted a cluster of mushrooms, which she quickly gathered and put in the basket on her back. Usually without slowing her pace, she collected handfuls of berries, kola nuts, and some green leaves. She did all this while apparently continuing to be aware of the location of everybody else, including the men, who were nowhere in sight. There was no shouting, but several times I saw Miasa pause to listen carefully for sounds I did not always hear or recognize. But I knew that at least a part of her apparent sense of direction was based on things and places familiar to her. To me, an outsider, the endless trees looked alike.

Each Mbuti band tended to spend its entire existence in one particular section of the forest, usually marked by natural boundaries such as streams, hills, and changes in the vegetation. In a lifetime of nomadic wandering through one's large but clearly defined territory, certain landmarks and locations would become established—the place where Sangu killed the elephant, the tree where Madada fell while getting honey, the sunny clearing where the animals come to eat the earth with the salt in it. To the Mbuti, these were street names and place names imprinted only on memory and were ever changing over the generations as new events occurred and old ones were forgotten. To be an Mbuti was the only way to know them all.

Miasa wore a G-string made of faded bark cloth as her only adornment, and like the other women, her feet were bare. In the irresponsible days of my youth, when I had hunted elephants for their ivory, I had envied my African companions for their ability to walk barefoot while hunting. The game in the Ituri was smaller but just as sensitive to the dramatic crunch of a dried leaf or the painfully loud snap of a twig. To be noisy now meant to disgrace oneself and to justify the warnings of the two women who had objected to my joining the ranks of the beaters.

The best way to do all the right things was to follow Miasa and do everything she did. I stopped to listen only when she listened, and walked only where she walked. I did not want to be the one to step on a piece of dried wood, and so kept an eye carefully on the path directly ahead. Momentarily distracted by the dappled light playing on the rippling, glossy surface of my companion's bare glutei maximi, I eventually did step on a twig, but Miasa was polite enough to ignore it.

At the place where we found the men silently setting up the nets, the women divided into two groups, each group keeping pace with its end of the combined net as it quickly grew again into a large half-circle. When the last net was tied in place, I followed Miasa as she quietly led her companions in a line through the forest. In a few moments we met the first of the other women coming from the opposite end of the net, and the trap was set.

For me, it was a truly unique experience. I had always hunted alone or with other men. Women were the beings who cooked what the men killed and brought back to camp. But here the hunt depended on the skill of the women and their knowledge of the psychology of the animals they hunted. The results at the net would thus in large measure reflect the efforts of the women and not just of the men who mindlessly butchered whatever animals the women sent their way. And if a hunt went badly and no animals were killed, the food the women industriously collected in their baskets during the hunt would be all there was, and it would be shared with the men.

Miasa glanced along the line of women and girls as she waited with them. Now everything depended on an antelope or two hiding somewhere among the trees between us and the men. In the distance a troop of baboons jabbered excitedly, then there was silence again. From somewhere I heard a single call that was the signal we waited for. With lusty shouts and the beating of sticks, the women simultaneously began their advance toward the distant net and the silent, waiting hunters.

I saw Miasa reach for something hiding beneath a bush. It was a baby mboloko antelope, apparently left by its mother when the shouting began. When we reached the net, the only antelope I saw killed was a female that was probably the baby's mother. Miasa carried the struggling baby to her husband, who promptly killed it with Miasa's own knife before putting it in his wife's basket, which she had left at the net. The baby's mother ended up in the basket of the wife of the hunter in whose net it had been killed. Apparently there had been another antelope, but it had somehow jumped the net and escaped.

When Kachelewa appeared, I suggested to him that we head back toward the camp. This pleased him because he did not care much for the hard work involved in hunting; this is probably why I found him in Epulu. But like Abeli, he had been reared in the forest and was just as skilled in its lore as the hunters we were leaving behind.

During the walk back to Camp Ekale, it was Kachelewa who first heard the distant sound of chopping. He stopped in his tracks and cocked his head to listen. "Honey," he said dramatically. "Somebody has found a honey tree." He looked at me expectantly.

"Let's go and eat some honey," I told him, wanting to witness the event.

Kachelewa took off with more energy than he had shown all day, plunging northward through the trees, away from the track we had been following. Stopping every few minutes, he would again locate the sound and dash off again. Watching his enthusiastic behavior, I wondered what he would say if he could see the dozens of glass jars of honey on display in the average modern supermarket. In a short time the chopping stopped, but happily we could now hear the sound of voices, and minutes later we came out in a clearing to find the two girls Kimbi and Makela sitting on a log beneath a large buttress-rooted tree. From high above us came the sound of two men talking. They were so far up the tree that they couldn't be seen from the ground. I sat beside the girls and watched Kachelewa begin to climb the hanging vines that led up to where the two men were. About thirty feet off the ground, he changed his mind and came back down to flirt with the girls instead.

Soon a basket lined with leaves was lowered on a rope of tree bark through the overhead greenery. It was half full of honeycombs, and Kachelewa dashed to hold a cupped leaf beneath it to catch the precious stream of leaking honey. Minutes later, the two youths who had performed the dangerous raid on a high-altitude bees' nest climbed down the vines to join us in the feast. The boys' names were Sefu and Pushipush, and it was soon apparent that Pushipush was unable to talk or even make recognizable sounds. He was in fact dumb, and possibly a deaf mute. He also had the only buckteeth I had seen in the Ituri forest, and I wondered if this had anything to do with his condition. He was about eighteen years old, unmarried, and as I would subsequently learn, a kind of camp clown. Nobody took him seriously, especially Kachelewa, who teased him mercilessly by forever imitating the pathetic animal sounds he made, although it is doubtful if Pushipush was fully aware of the teasing. On the other hand, when I later tested his hearing by shouting his name when he had his back to me, he stopped walking two out of three times and looked around at me with a puzzled expression on his face. On this scant evidence, I am forever left wondering whether he was partly deaf or if he was so accustomed to people not taking him seriously that he had learned to ignore the sincere but rare attempts to communicate with him.

When Pushipush produced a little rusted can and indicated with gestures and noises that he wanted some of the honey he had risked his life for, the others ignored him, and he was apparently too gentle to take it for himself. I hoped he had been clever enough to eat his share while still up in the tree.

Though Kachelewa had insisted that his friend was crazy, it was Pushipush we all followed without question as he unerringly led the way back to camp through the endless maze of trees, absently tapping a finger against his little rusted can as if it was a miniature drum.

This had been the second time in a week that I found honey being gathered in the Ituri. In the tropical Ituri forest, the presence of bees and their nests is constant despite a so-called "honey season." Only the quality and quantity of the honey may vary, depending on the seasonal flowering of certain trees, especially the mbau tree, which also produces a beanlike seed that both the Mbuti and the wild animals and even the fish in the river eat. The mbau bean is the same one that the Mbuti taught Stanley to eat when he was starving.

By midafternoon the hunters and women began arriving back at Camp Ekale. Several of the women carried mboloko in their baskets, and one young hunter proudly staggered back carrying a young yellow-backed duiker on his shoulders; next to the bongo, this is the largest species of antelope in the forest. It had been a good day's hunt, and the camp had a distinctively festive air about it. Both men and women returning from the hunt wore bunches of green leaves tucked into their belts as decoration. People laughed and shouted at one another across the camp, sometimes joking about events of the hunt, especially where somebody had missed an easy target or made a fool of himself in some way. But mistakes or not, there was an abundance of food and no need to hunt the next day.

Abeli came to me, blood spattered and happy. "There is much meat at Ekale, just like I told you," he said. "The people here are the best hunters in all the forest!"

I looked at the fires smoking beneath numerous antelope carcasses and saw his point. "Do you want to return to Epulu tomorrow?" I asked him jokingly.

Abeli shook his head vehemently. "Now it's better here at Ekale. We should stay in the forest!"

"So we can eat a lot of meat?"

Smilingly, Abeli agreed, then added more seriously, "Tonight may be the last night of the Molimo. There will be a great feast and much singing and dancing. The *Mangese* [elders] all say you will be welcome to join them at the *Kumamolimo* fire tonight."

Thunder echoed ominously across the forest from the east.

"Is the rain coming?" I asked, worried about a washed-out evening.

Abeli looked up through the trees at patches of blue sky and thought for a moment or two. "Maybe it will," he finally told me, still looking upward. "And maybe it won't," he added with a shrug as he dropped his gaze and walked off to join a couple of young women visiting the hut where he was sleeping.

I had noticed the Molimo basket hanging from a tree stump in the center of the camp. When we first arrived, some of our bananas had been put into it by Abeli. I thought that now would be a good time to make some kind of personal offering. And so, taking a few packs of cigarettes from my newly completed hut, I walked across to the Molimo basket and dropped them in. As an item otherwise unavailable in the forest, they would be a decidedly appreciated contribution toward the evening festivities.

Soon all the firewood and water had been collected for the evening, and the women began cooking meals for their families. This was the time when the girls and younger women prepared for their social evening. Sitting in groups according to age and friendship, they painted themselves and each other with the blackened juice of the kangay plant. Next to me, Kimbi was busy painting Makela's body, using only her finger to apply the black juice. She began on her buxom friend's breasts and arms, painting dots, lines, and circles that represented her own design. In the painting of bodies and bark cloth, the Mbuti have no rigid tribal patterns, and each woman paints whatever pleases her.

Makela had already painted stripes on her own lower legs. Now Kimbi was painting interesting designs on Makela's bare buttocks while she stood impassively waiting her turn to do the same for Kimbi. In time they would get around to doing each other's faces, using a delicate twig with which to paint fine, artistic lines. When all was finished, each had to assume that her facial makeup was as good as she hoped it would be, for they didn't possess mirrors. Even if a mirror had been available, the girls would still have painted each other's bodies and faces as a mark of friendship and affection, just as they groomed and removed lice from each other's hair.

Toward nightfall, embers were collected from the fires of every family and used collectively to build up the central fire called the Kumamolimo. This act symbolized the involvement and participation of every man, woman, and child in the Molimo festival. Later, the central fire was where the men of the Molimo met, and it was the focal point of the religious festival itself.

Again thunder rolled across the forest, and Makubasi looked up at the treetops as if hoping to catch a bird's-eye view of the ever-invisible horizon beyond. "The rain is coming, but it will pass that way!" he said, indicating a point north of us with a sweep of his arm. I hoped he was right.

By nightfall, everybody had eaten the basic evening meal, and the camp was a tiny island of glowing fires in an endless sea of darkened forest. It was the time of the aardvark and the leopard, of the trumpeting elephant and the screaming tree hyrax. It was also the time of the Molimo.

Abruptly, from the nearby forest came a loud, eerie sound resembling an elephant trumpet, but deeper and more melodic. It quickly changed moods from a roar to a trailing moan, only to become the cough of a prowling leopard. It was the Molimo trumpet.

Within moments, all the women, girls, and children had disappeared into the huts, leaving the men outside. Under no circumstances should the eyes of the women gaze upon the trumpet of the Molimo.

Now the trumpet sounded from another direction, even closer to the camp, and I remembered what I had previously learned about the Mbuti and the Molimo festival.

In contrast with the Sudanic and Bantu village cultivators of the Ituri, who worship their dead and believe that every bad happening, including sickness and death, is deliberately caused by some person or persons, known or unknown (who are considered witches or sorcerers), the Mbuti lead a comparatively carefree life and have relatively little to do with witchcraft, sorcery, or superstitious beliefs (although this has changed progressively over the years as the Mbuti increasingly adopt the villagers' beliefs in the supernatural, including a belief in the widespread existence of essentially antisocial and evil *mbolozi*, or witches).

If the Mbuti believe in a god, one form it may take is the magnificent world of the forest itself, which they think of in deified terms. They say they are the children of the forest, and that it is both their mother and father, for it gives them food, clothing, and shelter. They pray to it for good hunting and light fires in its honor. When bad hunting, illness, or misfortune strikes the band, or especially when somebody important to the community dies (as had recently occurred), the band may decide to hold a religious festival to mark the occasion. Some Mbuti call this festival the Molimo, and it may extend through each rainless evening for a month or more, or until conditions improve. The Efe Mbuti call the trumpet *Lusomba*.

The Molimo is an attempt to awaken the living and benevolent forest to the band's misfortune, and to make the forest a cheerful place once again. And so a most important part of the Molimo consists of singing daily to the forest. The Mbuti like to sing, and both men and women do so frequently—even more than their beloved dancing. But the Molimo is both a community festival and a kind of male religious society—just as the *Elima* festival is a women's affair—and only the men may sing the special Molimo songs to the forest.

For perhaps a half-hour I sat quietly listening to the Molimo trumpet as it moved from place to place among the trees around the camp. I strained to catch a glimpse of it, but couldn't see anything, not even the hunters who carried and played it.

Anjuway picked up the banja sticks from near the central fire and beat them together for a moment. The young hunter Madada then just as casually walked over to the drum hanging beside the Molimo basket. He took it and beat a few notes before carrying it to the fire in order to dry and stretch its skin with the flames.

Anjuway absently beat the banja sticks once more, and Madada replied with a staccato burst on the drum. Anjuway beat the banja sticks again, and this time the drum replied and did not stop. It was the signal for the Molimo dancing to begin, and the women and children began to reappear from the huts.

The Molimo trumpet was subdued for now, but it would return later to dominate the most religious part of the night's events. Meanwhile, from time to time we could hear it waiting, its impatient growl sounding in the dark forest.

I joined the men at the central fire around which the dancing and singing had started. Kachelewa and Abeli were already there, and I sat down across from them and beside Makubasi and the Mangese, his fellow elders. I had brought my own three-stick chair.

The scene was barely illuminated by the fire until somebody lit a piece of resin. Obtained from the mbeli tree, it was about the size of a child's fist and represented the Mbuti's most advanced—and only—form of artificial lighting after the ordinary wood fire. Placed on the damp earth, its flickering yellow flame illuminated the eager dancers and threw their shadows grotesquely against the trees and rising smoke. There was no age barrier among those participating, and anybody who wanted to dance joined in the circle of people who shuffled or gamboled around the fire.

Although traditional Mbuti dancing usually moves around a fire in the same circular counterclockwise direction, individual expression was not discouraged, and, depending on the opportunity, frequently took the form of the erotic dancing that the Mbuti are known for. A hunter strutted and jerked in obvious imitation of the basic sex act. Another playfully clasped a woman dancer to him in a momentary embrace that was more than suggestive. And soon the young men began to dance none but erotic dances. But there were other interests. Sitting next to me, Makubasi took his turn to inhale bangi smoke from a four-foot pipe made from the stem of a banana leaf. To keep it alight, he had placed burning embers on top of the large bowl. Next to Makubasi, another elder held his bright-eyed little grand-daughter on his lap. She climbed down and began to imitate the dancers with captivating charm. A woman scooped up the naked little girl and danced with her once around the fire before depositing her again into the lap of her grandfather.

Kimbi and Makela, the band's two most eligible single girls of marriageable age, finally made their entrance. Makela was tall for an Mbuti and, like her friend, was probably about fourteen years old. Kimbi was about four and a half feet tall and possessed the light golden skin sometimes found among the Mbuti, and especially among the more western groups of African Pygmies I had visited. Both girls were fully developed, mature young ladies with full, pouting breasts that had yet to feed an infant. They were both attractive enough to turn any man's head and were proudly aware of it.

From time to time, the Molimo trumpet called out from the forest, alternately plaintive and threatening. But the elders sitting around the fire shouted at it to go away. And so it waited, with increasing impatience, it seemed.

A woman brought a pot filled with the meat of a red duiker antelope, which the Mbuti in this part of the forest call *sondo*. She put it on the Molimo fire to cook. When ready it would be eaten only by the men of the Molimo. I looked up to see the elder Yauli dancing with the furry skin of a genet hanging from his hand. He seemed to enjoy dangling it in front of people's faces then nonchalantly passing it to another hunter, who danced with it in much the same way.

The piece of resin had long since burned out, and despite the repeated rearrangement of the fire, the dancing was easier to hear than see in the poor light. But then the moon came out from behind the clouds, sending moonbeams streaming through the rising smoke of the fires to light the sort of scene that had remained unchanged for thousands of years. Each hut had its smoldering fire, and at one of them a group of youths were doing their own erotic dance to the music of the Molimo drum. But all too soon the clouds again obscured the moon and everything was once more thrown into darkness. Someone tried to rearrange the fire to give better light, but the pot of sondo meat blocked the flames. Finally, Makubasi called for somebody to light another piece of resin.

It was no more than the light of a single candle, yet in the stygian darkness of the deep forest, the sputtering resin lit the scene like an Olympic torch. Shadows materialized as warm, living bodies with recognizable faces. Acts of comic and erotic behavior were once more appreciated by the onlookers and fellow dancers. It was as if the lights had been turned on again.

To celebrate the moment, a woman wearing only the slenderest of G-strings stepped out of the crowd and for a moment playfully danced alone, with her bare buttocks swaying and twitching sensuously directly over the flickering resin light. It was the Mbuti equivalent of stepping into the spotlight. She was a camp matron, yet for a wonderful moment she proudly enjoyed being a girl again, perhaps telling the world that even with repeated motherhood and the grinding daily hard work, she was still a very sexy lady.

About four hours after sunset the Molimo trumpet began to sing more loudly, leaving no doubt that its time had come. Now the men were quiet and did not shout at it to go away. The women, girls, and children retired to their huts for the night, where they would sleep or be respectfully silent for as long as the Molimo songs were heard. Only the hunters and older men remained sitting around the sacred Molimo fire.

For many minutes the Molimo trumpet sang alone in the forest. It sang in many moods—fiercely, soothingly, plaintively—until one of the men by the fire responded by starting to quietly beat the banja sticks. Then the unseen trumpet stopped its animal noises and began to sing a haunting Mbuti melody, not with words, but with its own ethereal sound. The men at first responded by humming the same melody and then by singing the words. A hunter quietly began to play the drum in unobtrusive harmony with the trumpet and singers. And so began the most sacred songs of the Mbuti Pygmies, played and sung to their beloved forest home. It is an event that exceedingly few outsiders have been privileged to witness, and for me it was a profound experience never to be forgotten.

At no time did any of the men look toward the forest. Instead, they gazed into the fire that symbolized the Molimo and the forest itself. Sometimes the trumpet led the singing, with the men responding in chorus, and at other times the men seemed to play the lead and the trumpet responded in turn.

The sound of the trumpet was absolutely unique in my experience. Its sonorous voice struck a responsive chord deep in my psyche, reaching a part of my mind that may have been dormant for millennia. The trumpet became part of me and I was part of it. The sound was hypnotic. The voice of the Molimo demanded attention and could not be ignored. It echoed and reechoed through the forest, its deep, resonant growl swelling to a magnificent Mbuti melody, then mellowing to a gentle lullaby as the hunters responded.

The trumpet suddenly sounded at the very edge of the camp, but the men continued to sing without pause. Then a group of hunters rushed from the darkness of the forest into the firelight, carrying a long object between them that was entirely covered with a cloak of leafy branches. They encircled the fire and the singing men several times before putting their burden on the ground beside Makubasi. The old man scooped up a handful of hot ashes from the fire and, pulling aside a cluster of green leaves, rubbed them on the smooth surface of the Molimo trumpet that was momentarily naked and exposed. It was a blackened length of bamboo at least six feet long and about three inches wide. Again picking up the trumpet, the hunters carried it among us so that we were each touched by its raiment of trailing leaves. Then, in a moment, the hunters and trumpet had disappeared once more among the trees.

The men at the fire continued to sing, and the trumpet could still be heard, but from farther and farther away as it carried the message of goodwill from its children into the heart of the forest.

The Molimo trumpet was heard the next morning, occasionally growling not far from camp. After much discussion among all the men present, I was eventually accorded the great privilege of being taken into the forest to see and photograph the trumpet itself. It and the man playing it were completely covered in leafy branches, and only after a heated argument among those present were the branches removed so that I could take a photograph. I was not alone in thinking that what I was doing was sacrilegious.

Regrettably my stay among the Mbuti net hunters of Ekale would soon come to an end. I had been continuously in the equatorial forests of the People's Republic of the Congo/Zaire for four months now, walking long distances and living in rugged conditions. I had been successfully attacked by a thousand insects and itched all over, including places difficult to reach.

Abeli, Kachelewa, and Anziani accompanied me on the long walk back to the road at Epulu. I gave Abeli and Kachelewa the money we had previously agreed on, and also gave Abeli a safari jacket which I had bought in Nairobi. It was too big for him and came down almost to his knees, but he was very proud of it; indeed, it was the very first jacket he had ever owned. Because she had uncomplainingly carried the heaviest load in her basket, I bought a length of imported cloth for Anziani which delighted her, especially as no arrangements had been made to pay her anything at all. The cloth cost more than double the value of the money I had agreed to give to her husband Kachelewa, who had carried nothing.

I would leave the Ituri at this time, but would return within the year to a remote section of the forest where I would camp with a band of Efe Mbuti archers. Besides wanting to compare them with the net hunting Mbuti, I wished to study their relationship with the Lese village cultivators, as I believed it came closest to resembling the Mbuti-villager relationship at the time the cultivators first arrived in the forest.

# 4

## The Efe and The Lese

If the east-west road through the Ituri is in poor condition, the only road running northward through its center has become impassable at its southern end and has been closed indefinitely. The northern part is so little used that grass grows between the twin tracks made by the few missionary, trading, and government vehicles that use it. In this part of the country there are no private vehicles.

I traveled north on this road to the village of Nduye, a place even more remote than Epulu. Here the village cultivators are the Sudanic Lese Negroes, and they associate with bands of Efe Mbuti Pygmies who live in the surrounding forest. This is the area in which I was continuing my pilgrimage among the people I considered among the most fascinating and rarest in all the world.

What does one do to join a nomadic band of Efe Pygmies somewhere out there in the deep forest? My first step was to find somebody from such a band who might happen to be visiting the road. It took a day and a night, but eventually I found such an Efe (a term I shall interchange with the word Mbuti).

Boloko was one of the smallest Mbuti men I had ever seen,

being barely four feet tall. He was about eighteen years old and had an impish smile and infectious sense of humor that would make him an ideal traveling companion. He readily agreed to guide me to his relatives in the forest and had soon recruited three Mbuti friends to help carry the rice, palm oil, medicines, tape recorder, and other items I had brought. Most of the things I took into the forest with me were important for sustaining life and for sharing with my Mbuti hosts.

Boloko's friends were named Asani, Paligbo, and—the old man of the group—Kufako. Conversing in Kingwana, the region's lingua franca, we agreed on the amount I would pay each of them per day in the forest plus a special bonus I would give on returning safely back to the road. It was interesting to see how fairly they proportioned and carried the loads among themselves. With hardly a word, Boloko made straps from the stems of large mongongo plants and tied everything into bundles so that they could be carried on the back. Asani, who was young and the strongest, took the heaviest load, Paligbo, the second heaviest, and Boloko and Kufako took the lightest.

We started out on the long march into the forest with Boloko leading the way. In the first few hours, we passed through the villages of Maitatu and Mukonja, eventually coming to the large village of Andili, the home of Mulebaloti, the local Lese chief. Along the way we had crossed the Ukomba, Kitule, and Makalambi rivers by wading or using fallen trees as bridges. To the north we had caught a glimpse of the mysterious Mount Mukonja, rising out of the forest like a lonely sentinel guarding this endless land of trees. Boloko and his friends were always happy to provide me with local names for my ever-ready notebook, although I wonder now if anybody living more than a day's journey away from these spots would be interested.

The path we had been following so far was well used, but it only became comfortable when it left the blazing sun of the clearings and went beneath the trees. It would become more narrow and shaded after the agricultural village of Andili, which was the last Lese habitation we would see. Only the Mbuti lived beyond this point.

When we came to Andili, I was impressed with its two neat, orderly rows of leaf-roofed, mud-walled houses facing each other across a clean-swept central "avenue" of red earth. As cultivators, the people had long since cut down the forest around the village, leaving little shelter from the blazing equatorial sun.

In the shimmering heat, there was nobody in sight except two men sitting listlessly in the shade of the *baraza*, a central meeting place covered with a roof of banana leaves supported on poles. I greeted the two men and was invited inside, where I sat on one of several vacant chairs. Boloko and the others waited respectfully outside in the sun until I had started a conversation with the villagers, then they entered and quietly sat on the ground in the shade at the edge of the shelter with their backs against the upright poles. We had walked steadily for several hours through the heat of the day, and the chance to rest was welcome to us all.

Both these Lese villagers were much darker skinned than most of the Bila villagers I had seen. They were middle-aged and appeared to be important men in their community. After a polite interval, I asked if I might meet the chief, for I knew it was important to gain his approval to be in his area—and to live among his Mbuti. By then we had been joined by two more men, but an hour elapsed before Chief Mulebaloti himself appeared from a nearby house, where I suspect he had been sleeping.

The chief was a handsome, slender man of about sixty who was dressed in an ordinary shirt and long trousers and was barefooted. He sat on the chair beside me, and for several minutes no one spoke as a bowl of village-brewed beer was brought and passed among us. When I eventually told him of my plans to camp in the forest, he seemed puzzled as to why anybody would want to share the hard life of the Mbuti. Waving toward a nearby house that was just then being swept out by a young woman, he said I was welcome to sleep there and that there would be someone to fetch water and cook for me. I thanked him but stated firmly that I intended to stay with the Mbuti in the forest.

We departed soon after, leaving the chief and his men sitting quietly in the baraza with a fresh bowl of beer. Only when we were back in the friendly shade of the forest did the usually irrepressible Boloko smile again. He had enjoyed the visit and the excuse to sit with Chief Mulebaloti, but did not like having to remain silent for so long. Regrettably, the Lese had apparently considered extended social conversation with my traveling companions beneath them. Inadvertently, I had contributed to this by merely being there, for one way the villagers had shown respect toward me was by ignoring the Mbuti who came with me.

We reached the Mbuti-inhabited camp of Ndanji on the outskirts of Andili that evening before dark. There I met Boloko's grandmother, Dolengani, who was delighted to see her grandson but somewhat startled to meet me. There were nine huts and about twenty people living in Ndanji but the decay of the huts and the presence of chickens indicated that it was, in effect, an Mbuti-inhabited suburb of Andili. However, there were apparently other Mbuti camps farther into the forest, and I decided to walk to them the next day. But the following morning, Chief Mulebaloti sent word that he wanted to see me again. I didn't want to take the time, but I thought it prudent to walk back and meet him once more, as he demanded. Under modern law, a villager could no longer "own" an Mbuti, but the chief still had a real, if unofficial, power among the Mbuti in his area. Enlightened, well-meaning directives from the government in Kinshasa meant little when applied to a region one thousand miles away and unconnected by regular transportation.

It would have been unwise of me to ignore the fact that this was the chief's territory and that I was at his mercy. If he did nothing else, he might have attempted to influence the Mbuti in his area to be uncooperative and withdraw any support they might give me.

After the usual greetings and polite conversation, Mulebaloti handed me a note written in Kingwana, requesting a payment of twenty zaires (about seven dollars). I had given many such payments during my twenty years in Africa but never before to a written demand. It was a sign of the times, I thought as I walked to the edge of the village with the chief, where I gave him the money out of sight of his circle of elders. The written note indicated that he or one of his people had attended the Catholic mission school at Nduye.

Boloko and his friends didn't want to leave the good company they found in Ndanji, but I insisted on proceeding without delay. I bought two scrawny chickens and three tiny eggs, and we were on our way before noon. In the interests of trivia, I cannot resist mentioning that the word used by the local Mbuti to scare away camp chickens attempting to steal food is "Kissy! Kissy!" or sometimes just "Kiss! Kiss!"

An hour's walk through the forest north of Ndanji brought us at last to Camp Anditopi, which was too exposed to the broiling sun for my taste. But another hour's walk, during which we were soaked by a heavy rain, led us to the more shaded camp of Andibamba, and this is where I decided to stay if we were welcome. I let Boloko enter a little ahead of us so that the people wouldn't be startled by my unexpected appearance. He didn't have relatives there but knew some of the people.

As the rest of us entered the settlement, I counted ten huts, including three set apart from the others close to a picturesque stream. The man who greeted us seemed to speak for the people of Andibamba when he invited us to sit at the central fire. His name was Pano, and he was an energetic, skinny man of about fifty who was quick to smile and loved to talk. He sat with the camp's oldest man, Kambatoka, and with the camp capita, Mbute.

It was midafternoon and the women and girls of the camp began to arrive back with the foods they had been gathering all day in the forest. Their baskets mainly contained two kinds of mushrooms and a generous quantity of palm-oil nuts. The women were surprised to see me sitting at the camp fire, and questions and explanations were shouted back and forth amid some good-natured laughter.

They were strong and willing, these tiny Mbuti women, and they routinely gathered about 80 percent of the food consumed in a hunting camp of Mbuti archers. Indeed, from a woman's point of view, such nomadic communities could be more accurately called gathering or foraging camps. Even among the Mbuti net hunters, who kill much more game than these Mbuti archers, the women themselves become hunters and then contribute considerably more by carrying the heavy meat back to camp in their baskets in an unerring trek through miles of muddy, tangled rain forest. But if the sexual division of labor in acquiring food is flexible enough for the women to take part in the actual hunting, it's also flexible enough for the men to gather vegetable foods sometimes just as the women do. Even a hunter can't ignore a succulent patch of mushrooms he may stumble across and will find a way to carry them back to camp, especially if he has failed to kill an animal for its meat.

Yet most of the vegetable foods consumed in an Efe camp come from the cultivated crops of the Lese farmers. This is not always obtained by the Efe through bartering meat and honey from the forest. In a recent systematic study of "subsistence strategies" in the Ituri forest, Harvard anthropologists Robert Bailey and Nadine Peacock found that 68 percent of the cultivated foods acquired by the Efe was earned by laboring for the Lese in their villages and gardens. This laboring is done mostly by Efe women.

I watched Pano's wife, Bakira, who had earlier searched the forest all day for wild foods, walk into camp with an enormous burden of rain-soaked firewood that must have weighed almost as much as she did. The logs were tied together with bark rope and were supported on her bare back and head by a bark strap or tumpline. She gratefully let the heavy load drop beside her hut, and then went off to wash in the nearby stream and fetch water for the preparation of the evening meal. She was accompanied by two little girls, both of whom had carried heavy loads of firewood proportionate to their age.

A playful air current caused the smoke from the fire to drift into my face. Pano expertly located the offending piece of wood that alone caused the excessive smoke and carelessly threw it over his shoulder. Together with the other men, we discussed the local hunting and such things as the frequency of rainstorms and the advantages of mongongo leaves over banana leaves for the roofing of huts. After a while it was clear that Pano looked on the diversion I provided with genuine pleasure and arranged for me to sleep in an obliging relative's hut until a new one could be built for me. I felt just a little guilty that Boloko and his friends would sleep on the open ground around the communal fire the nights we were to stay here. It was the price they paid for not having relatives in Andibamba—and for not being a delicate, fragile Muzungu like myself.

Some anthropologists seem to expect that any group of people they choose to live among for a fieldwork project will be so honored by their presence that acceptance will be almost a right. The practical truth is that for an unknown outsider to be accepted by a host group is a privilege not to be taken for granted.

If the people to be studied are existing on a bare subsistence level (and even if they're not), it is hardly fair to expect them to provide hospitality and shelter, not to mention an intimate knowledge of their culture, without giving something in return. In the case of the Mbuti, I gave such things as food, medicines, limited medical treatment, knives, nylon line, and my companionship and affection. And when it comes to photography in a society where cameras are nonexistent, Polaroid pictures are especially appreciated, because they are given and not taken.

The Mbuti, like other hunting and gathering groups, practice a sharing reciprocity, which means that things are given or shared back and forth among them without anyone's necessarily expecting anything in return. Yet they can also switch to and appreciate a balanced reciprocity, such as in my own culture, where—except in a nuclear family—things are usually only given in exchange for other things.

On the material level, the people of Andibamba possessed almost nothing. I could have bought everything owned by these twenty-five people for just twenty-five dollars. For fifty dollars I could have bought the entire camp, huts and all. If Ndanji was a ramshackle suburb of the farming village of Andili, then Andibamba was just one step away from similar acculturation. It was far enough into the forest for the women to find mushrooms and other edibles, yet not far enough for the hunters to find an adequate number of game animals. Occasional troops of monkeys wandering by chance to the edge of the camp provided much of the meat killed by the hunters, who rarely shot anything at all. This was not a permanent village campsite of the kind maintained by the Mbuti at the edge of a village for those months when they're not in the forest hunting. Neither was it a nomadic hunting camp in the forest, ready to move to another site when the game around it became scarce.

In imitation of the village cultivators, a patch of forest had been laboriously cleared, and four banana shoots had been planted where the sun could reach them. Nearby stood a few young papaya trees grown from seeds.

From my personal experience of growing these fruits in other parts of tropical Africa, I knew that Andibamba would have to wait eighteen months before reaping a crop. This Mbuti band clearly represented a nomadic hunting and gathering culture in transition. For these twenty-five people, nomadism had effectively ceased and hunting had become an occasional occupation of just a few of the men. Only the continued, daily gathering efforts of the women, and whatever foods were obtained in exchange for laboring in the villages, kept the people alive.

I would stay here for only a few days before moving on to a more traditional Mbuti hunting camp deeper in the forest. Yet Andibamba was of great human interest. This little Mbuti community beside a stream in the Ituri forest was in the process of doing what most of our ancestors began to do ten thousand years ago, when they too discovered agriculture and abandoned their nomadic ways to settle in villages. If all goes well, Andibamba may one day become established as a village, and within a few centuries could conceivably grow into a town. In that case success will be measured over the years by the amount of their beloved forest they cut down in the name of farming.

Yet, interestingly, the sometimes tangled, secondary growth that eventually replaces the original primeval forest cut down by the villagers (and by enterprising, would-be Mbuti farmers) appears ultimately to sustain a greater wild animal population that makes it possible to hunt without having to walk long distances into the forest. I wrote of this phenomenon in a previous work (*Black Elephant Hunter,* 1960) in which I described the prevalence of the common grey duiker antelope near the gardens of the Bemba and Bisa tribes in Zambia. As a game animal important for its meat, I always found it near the villages and seldom if ever in remote, uninhabited areas of the Zambian forests.

Meanwhile, here I was sitting in an Mbuti camp that was caught between two worlds. It would soon be night, when the only light would come from the flickering flames of the fires and, if the sky was clear, from the stars. I had seen water being brought from the stream and firewood being shared. The cooking pots were steaming, and anyone who intended to stay in Andibamba that night was already in the camp, for nobody willingly traveled through the forest after dark. When the twelve-hour tropical night descended it was like being cut off from the rest of the world by a giant, impenetrable black wall as wide as the forest and as high as the sky.

By the time the women had started to prepare the evening meal, it was apparent that there was no meat at Andibamba. Nobody had recently killed any kind of animal, so for food everyone depended on a few bananas from the villagers and what the women had brought back from the forest—the mushrooms and a few edible roots, insects, and seeds. Boloko, with his bright, inquisitive eyes, was sitting expectantly by my side, and I told him to kill the two chickens we had brought and give one each to Bakira, the wife of Pano, and to Shifa, the wife of Mbute, the capita. Both these women had indicated they would be kind enough to cook for us. I also gave enough rice for everybody in the camp. Along with some of the salt and palm oil I had brought, we would all eat a reasonable meal with at least a taste of chicken. What I provided wasn't much for the hospitality and knowledge I might receive in return. And besides, I could not sit there and consume a veritable banquet while my hosts had little to eat.

Mealtimes are variable in an Mbuti camp, and tonight the

people would eat later than usual. A little boy and girl fell asleep before the meal was ready. They lay in each other's arms on some leaves beside the fire, their bare bodies exposed to the chilly night air. Their grandmother, Matalulu, left her rice-cooking chores for a moment to gently place a large piece of bark cloth over them.

During and after the shared meal, Pano adopted the role of storyteller, with an attentive audience listening to his every word. He told his stories with great drama and irresistible humor. He had an extraordinary ability to make sound effects and to mimic the people he talked about, causing his audience to roar with laughter. But it had been a long day, and while he was still talking, people began to wander off to their huts or to smooth a place on the ground to lie on close to the fire for the night.

By 10:30 P.M. everybody was in his sleeping place and the camp was quiet. I have seldom heard an Mbuti snore, and this is probably because they almost never sleep on their backs. When I have asked those Mbuti I have known best why they sleep only on their side, I was told that the entire camp will ridicule anybody who makes animal noises by snoring. The only sounds that night were from the darkened forest, a persistent owl calling to another in the far distance and a noisy tree hyrax* occasionally giving its unearthly, terrifying scream. Suddenly, thunder rolled ominously across the primeval land, and even the crickets were quiet in the expectant silence that followed. In the darkness of the night, all creatures, human and nonhuman, waited in dread for the blinding, battering rain that might come their way, their only protection the dancing leaves of the forest.

I stayed at Andibamba for only a week, but long enough to observe some of the interaction between the Mbuti and the Lese villagers of Andili. First, there was the existence of the village-recognized capitas. The camps of Ndanji, Anditopi, and Andibamba each had one, and just two days after my arrival all three of these fellows came to where I sat outside my hut. Their

---

*Dendrohyrax arboreus,* of the order Hyracoidea. Rabbit-sized animals renowned for being the nearest living relative of the elephant.

manner clearly indicated it was not a social call, and apparently they had decided that as capitas they should each receive a payment from me.

"Why?" I asked curiously.

"Because we are the capitas of the places you are visiting," they told me. I gave one or two good reasons why I should not pay, but no argument would have convinced these men to abandon their scheme.

"How much do you want?" I inquired. They shuffled their feet uncomfortably.

"Five zaires each," they said reasonably enough.

"Will you want more money another time?" I asked as sternly as I could.

"No, no," they assured me quickly. "We won't ask you again."

I had paid to have my hut built and for any other services along the way. I did not have to pay them anything more, but I also knew that in the circumstances their continued cooperation was desirable. There was a lot of forest between me and the road.

I paid them each the five zaires they demanded, and the subject never came up again. I was against the payments on principle, but for a very small sum I had maintained and even elevated their official status in the eyes of the local people, for it was unlikely they had ever been paid like this before. But in true Mbuti fashion the matter seemed to be forgotten within moments, and no trace of embarrassment remained.

Later, I was sitting at the fire with Pano when he muttered something about "those people again." I looked up to see two village men walk out of the forest and approach us. Suddenly the camp was silent and the children stopped playing. It was obvious the two men were not welcome, but with a scowl Pano got up from his stool and the tallest of the villagers sat down on it without a word of greeting or even a grunt of acknowledgment. Silently, Pano brought a stool for the other villager and one for himself.

For thirty minutes the conversation was partly in Kingwana and partly in the Lese language, and seemed to be about nothing

Painting bark cloth.

"Stick" seat.

Woman sleeping on traditional bed.

Happy gathering taking shelter from rain.

Hunter with piece of honeycomb from nest of wild bees.

Picking mushrooms.

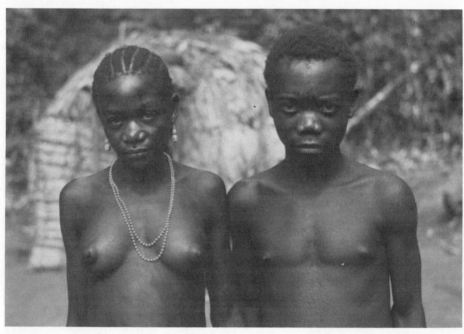

MBUTI FACES.

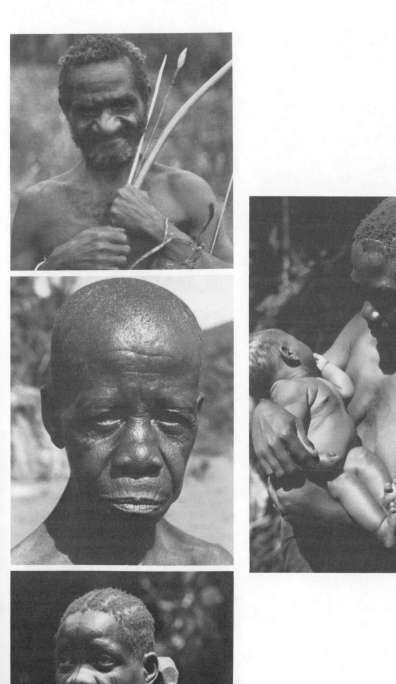

Smoking bangi (marijuana).

of great importance until the real purpose of the visit was finally mentioned: the two men wanted me to photograph them.

I told them I had very little film left, which was true, but they did not seem convinced. After a while I went into my hut, where I was followed by Pano. "If you give them a photo, they'll go away," he whispered pleadingly. I wondered if Pano simply did not want their company, or perhaps wished to make himself welcome on his next visit to Andili, or both. I went outside and again sat at the fire where Mbute and Kufako were still sitting with the now silent visitors.

Pano followed me and broke the tense silence by ordering the newly married teenage wife of his son to sweep the ground around us. The distraction was also a mark of respect, mainly for the benefit of the villagers, and everybody watched critically as the pretty girl bent double with a short, leafy branch to sweep the dirt away from around our feet. She wore a newly painted bark cloth with both red and black designs, and her legs and buttocks had been newly painted by a friend.

Unexpectedly, the taller villager sitting beside me stood and took the broom from the girl and vigorously began to sweep the ground himself. There were polite if surprised exclamations of appreciation from those watching him doing women's work, but after a brief demonstration, the man threw the broom on the ground and returned to his seat. The girl respectfully picked it up again to finish the job, but with no change in pace or technique.

Pano's giving his seat to the villager and then ordering the girl to sweep the ground was to show respect for the Lese visitors. When the villager took the broom, it was a symbolic gesture showing respect for me, but at the expense of the Mbuti's pride, for the act implied that the villager was my host and that the camp was his camp, the Mbuti his Mbuti.

I decided that if the villager was so anxious to have his picture taken, I would do it. I photographed him together with his companion, and a short time later they departed. When Pano said he was glad they were leaving, everybody laughed so loudly that I knew the villagers heard them.

When I asked Pano and the others if they liked the villagers, there was general agreement that nobody liked them. But when I asked if they would prefer to live in the forest without the villagers, there was not one who thought this an attractive idea. On our further discussing the relationship, it emerged that the Mbuti attached much value to the ever-present gardens of the villagers, where the cassava, plantains, bananas, tobacco, and bangi came from. If they were lucky, the Mbuti would drink a little palm wine or banana beer, and sometimes an individual Mbuti would receive an article of used clothing, an iron arrowhead, or a knife. But it also seemed that there was a desirable sense of belonging to an established farming village, a place where exotic things could be seen and sometimes acquired, where a strolling visitor could greet and be greeted and exchange gossip. To take the village away would be like taking away the local town from the rural population of our American West, especially before the advent of radio and television.

"But what did the villagers get from the Mbuti in return?" I asked those around the fire. "They want our girls for wives because our girls don't have venereal sickness like the village women," one man claimed (a remark commonly heard in the Ituri, especially where the Lese are concerned). "Many of their girls can't have babies because of this sickness, but our girls are healthy and give them many children."

Others mentioned the work the Mbuti did for the villagers in helping to clear the forest for more gardens, and the gathering of saplings and leaves for house building. Mbute reminded everybody of the mushrooms and other forest things provided by their wives. The hunters told of the meat that had been shared with Andili in the past, especially when an elephant had been killed two years earlier.

When I asked who got the most from whom, Pano said the villagers got the most because the Lese men sometimes took Mbuti girls as wives, yet never gave Lese girls in exchange.

"How much does a villager give for an Mbuti girl?" I asked.

Pano shook his head. "Maybe some bananas and a cooking pot," he said in disgust. "They give much more for a Lese girl."

"Why do you not refuse your girls?" I asked curiously.

At first nobody volunteered an answer, but eventually one man said that having a girl marry a villager meant more food from that villager's garden for the girl's family, who visit her from time to time. And besides, he added, the girls like to live in the big huts of the villagers.

"What would happen if you did refuse?" I asked.

Mbute, the capita, shrugged. "We might not be given any more food from the garden of the man we refused, and we would be less welcome in Andili."

"Then we would just take the bananas anyway!" Pano smiled.

Everybody laughed and began to talk of other things.

It was a peaceful moment with few distractions, and it seemed an ideal time and place to conduct an experiment I had wanted to try for some time. I put a special prerecorded cassette in my tape recorder and played it to the group sitting around the fire with me. It was a recording I had made when visiting an isolated group of Pygmies in what is today known as the People's Republic of the Congo, about a thousand miles west of where we now sat in the Ituri forest of northeastern Zaire. I had asked those Bayaka Pygmies to sing, and their singing is what I recorded.

Nobody except myself at the fire that evening had any advance knowledge of what was on the tape or of where it had been recorded. But within moments of my starting the tape, my Mbuti companions around the fire that night in Andibamba had eagerly recognized their fellow Pygmies from the west by identifying them as *Bambuti,* the collective name all Mbuti call themselves.

Giant mile-wide rivers and dozens of unfriendly tribes with as many languages have effectively separated the Mbuti from their western cousins for centuries, perhaps millennia. Yet both groups had somehow remained unacculturated enough to retain the unique sounds of Pygmy song, which had probably once been common to most if not all Pygmies in the great forest lying between eastern Uganda and the Atlantic Ocean. The Ituri is the easternmost part of this vast area.

The Mbuti have been linguistically divided by the Bantu and Sudanic peoples, whose languages they appear to have adopted at the expense of losing their own. Yet amid the dialectal differences, a peculiar intonation continues to characterize all Mbuti speech. Whatever findings future language studies may reveal, my experiment with the tape recorder reinforced the hypothesis that the various Pygmy groups now scattered throughout central and west equatorial Africa were once a single people with a common origin and culture. Yet just where and how they fit into the fragmented picture of early man in Africa may always remain a tantalizing mystery. The Belgian ethnomusicologist Benoit Quersin, whom I met once in the Ituri recording Mbuti music and singing, said that Pygmy sounds are different from anything else in Africa, or anywhere else for that matter.

In almost any discussion of the Mbuti Pygmies, questions are inevitably asked about the Mbuti-villager relationship. On such occasions I must explain that this aspect of Mbuti life in the Ituri forest varies, depending on the group and the place.

The band of net hunting Mbuti I camped with near Epulu hunted so efficiently that the value of their catch at the net often exceeded the value of the cultivated foods they required from the village farmers over a given number of days. Only generations of conditioning and a lack of interest in balanced reciprocity—in other words, poor business sense—kept the Mbuti hunters from becoming at least as wealthy as the villagers. In an area where livestock consists mainly of occasional goats and emaciated chickens, venison is a valuable product. Among the villagers there are professional meat traders who periodically visit the camps of the Mbuti net hunters to buy smoke-dried meat by the carcass, much of which goes on trucks to centers as far away as Kisangani to be sold for prices perhaps ten times higher than the Mbuti receive. In fact, if antelope and elephants become rare and endangered in the Ituri, it will be because non-Mbuti meat and ivory traders encourage the Mbuti hunters to kill more animals than they need for their own use.

Such Mbuti are well off during the months they hunt, and

are relatively independent of the villagers when they stay at Epulu. Some of them have even started their own gardens there in an attempt to produce their own cultivated foods.

At Andibamba my Efe Mbuti hosts presented a less prosperous picture, mainly because their primary hunting tool was the bow and arrow and not the hunting net. Even if this camp were moved farther into the forest, and the men hunted regularly, they could seldom kill more than they needed for their own use.

If some successful Mbuti net hunters have a symbiotic relationship of mutual exploitation with the village cultivators, the Efe Mbuti archers—who may well comprise a third or even half of the total Mbuti population—have a relationship that is perhaps not as pleasing to them or the villagers.

There has been much written about this aspect of Mbuti life, but not all of it explains the fundamental situation, without which there would be no relationship as we know it. Stripped of all textbook jargon and theory, the Mbuti-villager relationship is generally based on one of the most common principles of organized human behavior: those with the least (the Mbuti) are attracted to those with the most (the villagers).

When the Bantu and Sudanic peoples originally migrated into the Ituri they may well have found the Mbuti living much as they had for thousands of years. There are no historical records, but it is thought the newcomers introduced the bow and arrow, the hunting net, and even the basenji dog. And since the Mbuti don't know how to make fire to this day, it's possible the newcomers introduced that too, along with the use of iron, and clay pots for cooking and holding water. Then there were the exotic crops from the cultivators' gardens.

To the Mbuti, whose most sophisticated tool may have been a knife made of split bamboo and whose diet may not usually have included anything larger than insects, snakes, and the smallest animals, these were items that soon became necessities.

One way to get bananas was to steal them from the village plantations, which the Mbuti do to the present day. But eventually each scattered Mbuti band chose to attach itself to a host village, no matter what its tribe or language. In so doing, it gained access to every material thing the villagers had to offer, including iron knives and axes, exotic foods, and of course the village itself, an important center for their sense of belonging.

For their part, the villagers established a source of meat and honey without having to hunt for it, and the sometimes fierce little Mbuti could anyway be important allies in the event of war with neighboring tribes. Besides, to have or to "own" Mbuti was—and still is—more prestigious than not owning them.

Then as today, the villagers were prosperous only in contrast with the Mbuti, who owned nothing. The truth is that most villagers continue to be barely one step ahead of the Mbuti on the economic scale and actually seem relatively poverty-stricken compared with the average European. A knowledge of iron working and agriculture did not automatically elevate them to a life of silks and fine laces. Until recent times they wore bark cloth, if they wore clothing at all. Yet with dried mud instead of leaves for the walls of their huts, their homes were snug and warm, if, again, only one step ahead of the Mbuti. As subsistence farmers they still do not always have enough food for themselves, much less for a band of thieving Mbuti. Bailey and Peacock estimate that the average annual income per Lese household is less than fifty U. S. dollars. "Indeed," they say, "the Lese are generally recognized by the people of other tribes as being . . . impecunious due in large part to the draining relationship they maintain with the Efe." Bailey and Peacock also present a hypothesis that questions whether the Efe or any other Pygmy population could ever have existed independently of agriculture in the tropical rain forest of central Africa, and they question the "conventional wisdom" among anthropologists that Pygmies are the original inhabitants of the African tropical rain forest. Elsewhere Bailey makes the interesting statement that "The relationship between villagers and Mbuti . . . has existed for at least 2000 years." Only an archaeological study may one day provide empirical evidence of this, and Bailey indicates that such a study is being contemplated by Harvard University.

Because it is unlikely that the Mbuti hunting and gathering culture would have developed *after* a relationship was formed with farming peoples, I would ask where the Mbuti were located and what they were doing before developing such a relationship? Presumably they were separate, successful hunters and gatherers *somewhere* before becoming associated with the cultivators.

However, the villagers' folklore of their own background says that when they first arrived in the forest the Mbuti were already there. And there is as yet no convincing argument to say that Pygmies were not the original inhabitants of the forest (all the way across the great Congo basin to the Atlantic coast), or that the forest's natural, uncultivated products could not have adequately nourished them before the introduction of cultivated foods, iron, cooking pots, and even fire itself. It is perhaps significant that Stanley credited the Mbuti (and not the agricultural villagers) with providing him and his men with food when they were starving in the Ituri. This particular sustenance was specifically an uncultivated vegetable food. Again, while the Ituri is not as rich in plant species as the Amazon basin, the Mbuti hunt at least forty known animal species, with many others yet undocumented. The more common game animals include eight species of antelopes and about ten kinds of monkeys.

Although there have always been skilled hunters among the villagers, especially where there are no available Mbuti, they are often protein-starved and value the game meat sporadically provided by the Mbuti. There are recorded cases of cannibalism among the tribes of northeastern Zaire in this century, and the Lese particularly had a reputation for eating human flesh. But such cases apparently involved the rituals of secret societies and did not necessarily indicate a need for protein.

Although the villagers even now continue to think of the Mbuti as inferior beings, the children they father from Mbuti wives are gladly accepted into the tribe—even if the mother may one day be sent back alone to join her nomadic relatives in the forest when she becomes old and unattractive. Historically there has thus been a one-way flow of Mbuti genes out of the forest, as village girls are socially unavailable to Mbuti men. In this way the gene pool of the Mbuti has probably remained relatively "pure" over the years. In the presence of villagers the Mbuti are usually polite enough. But back in their forest hunting camps they refer to them as animals. For generations both sides have constantly schemed to get the most from the other, with the Mbuti frequently on the winning side, if only because they usually have the least to give.

One result of this often one-sided association is that each Mbuti family has come to acknowledge a specific individual among the villagers whom some call *kpara,* or owner. It is usually a permanent and even hereditary ownership, or at least the kpara would like to think so. But the ever-changing composition or flux of Mbuti bands, and of individual nuclear families, can make ownership claims difficult. The Mbuti get married, separate, remarry, have rows, and go to live with different relatives just like any other people.

Technically, the Mbuti are not slaves, although they acknowledge being owned. Nor are they serfs, for they are free to come and go as they please, and may even change their allegiance to another village.

And so the Mbuti-villager relationship is commonly seen as arrogant paternalism of the villagers and apparent servitude of the Mbuti. But the imagination of the cultivators who invaded the Ituri went beyond the practical. With an already established economic advantage, they eventually would further attempt to subjugate the Mbuti by imposing political and religious sanctions on them. But the circumcision of the Pygmy boys, or attempts to arrange marriages, would have little effect on the Mbuti once they had left the village and were back in the sanctuary of their forest where only they were masters.

Even today there are still bands of Mbuti hunters and gatherers living nomadically in the depths of the forest, their ancient way of life little affected by the outside world. I determined to find such a band, one that was not living anywhere near a large settlement such as Nduye or Epulu. It was while I was being driven on the road south of Nduye, far from anyplace marked on the map, that I located such a band quite by chance.

It happened when I stopped to talk with a young Efe Mbuti

couple I overtook on the road. When I asked where they were going, they told me they were returning to their camp, a day's walk into the forest. The young man's name was Sukali, and he couldn't have been more than eighteen years old. Like his wife he wore only a strip of bark cloth. He was lithe, muscular, and with a bow and quiver hanging from his shoulder, looked very much the traditional Mbuti hunter at his best. His wife, a pretty girl named Ndasu, was much younger, perhaps fifteen years old. They were too recently married to have had children.

Further questioning revealed that their band was living in a hunting camp far removed from the village with which they were associated, a village that in any case was too small to appear on a map. Such a hunting band was exactly what I had been searching for, and I was delighted when Sukali agreed to take me there. We all drove together through the forest until we came to a small roadside clearing containing about seven huts. This, Sukali told me, was the nearest point to his people's camp in the forest. I soon arranged with one of the Lese farmers who lived there for a place to sleep and a means to store the food and other things I had brought.

I then paid everything I owed to my driver, a man who had never been in the area before, telling him I would hitch a ride on a truck when I wanted to leave. At first he was surprised that I should want him to abandon me in such a desolate place. But he soon shrugged his acceptance of the plan, and after helping me move my things into a nearby hut, he was on his way back down the narrow track which some euphemistically called a road. For a few moments I watched with mixed emotions as he disappeared from sight, my severed link with the outside world. I knew he probably wouldn't see another vehicle for hours on such a little-used road.

This, I told myself solemnly, is true dedication in the cause of social anthropology, or was it foolhardiness in the face of better judgment? I supposed the answer would depend on whether I ever returned from the forest. Sukali and Ndasu shared my hut that night, and the following morning we together began the long walk into the forest world of the Mbuti Pygmies.

# 5

## Camp Tupi

Blood dripped from Mangoma's hands and his face distorted with rage. He was angry with Asumali, and becoming more angry every minute. Both men stood over the remains of a butchered antelope, a gory part of which Mangoma shook in Asumali's unflinching face. "It was my arrow that killed the animal," Mangoma shouted, "yet you gave the worst piece to my wife!"

"It's not the worst piece," Asumali protested with infuriating calm. "And besides, two arrows hit the animal at the same time, and it was Arumbu's dog that followed the animal when it ran off."

By now everybody in the camp had stopped whatever they were doing to watch and listen. It had been some time since such human drama had come to this Mbuti hunting camp deep in the Ituri forest.

The father of three teenage children, Mangoma was a powerfully built, almost squat Mbuti hunter who had filed teeth and often wore a porcupine quill through the cartilage of his nose. He was usually quiet and good-natured. Now he was not only angry, but plainly outraged. He flung his piece of raw meat on the ground and wildly began to jump on it. Then he turned to the other people of Camp Tupi, seeking their sympathy.

"Did I not kill the animal and deserve a better part?" he shouted, glaring from face to face, demanding an answer.

Only his loyal wife, Lehilehi, spoke up in his favor, but it was enough support to goad Mangoma to even greater fury. Turning again to the attack, he waved his fist in Asumali's face. "You are the animal, Asumali," he yelled, "not the thing on the ground. I killed the wrong animal!"

Asumali ignored the insult by turning to walk away, but Mangoma jumped into his path and delivered the greatest insult he could think of. He tore off his stained, sweaty bark cloth and flung it at Asumali's feet. "There," he screamed, "that's what you can eat—the cloth from the hunter who killed the animal!" And he stormed off stark naked to sulk in his hut, followed by his wife Lehilehi. For a few moments there was complete silence in the camp, then each person drifted back to whatever he or she had been doing when the row started. I have never seen a bark-cloth G-string washed, from the time it's made until it's finally discarded months later in the humid rain forest. Mangoma had invented a truly great insult, indeed.

It was the first serious row I had seen since my arrival in Camp Tupi—Buffalo Camp—a week earlier with Sukali and Ndasu. It had been a long walk into the forest, but this camp of Efe Mbuti bow-and-arrow-hunting Pygmies was everything I hoped it would be. They told me I was the first white man ever to stay with them in the forest, which was hardly surprising considering its remoteness from any place important enough to be on the map. Indeed, to their younger generation, a white man was a strange and exotic pink-white creature with straight hair who looked quite human but was rarely seen, and then usually in a vehicle passing along the distant road.

I sat at the central fire with some of the men, including Ndeke, an elderly widower who had become my good friend and counselor. He was gazing thoughtfully into the flames. "You know," he said quietly to the group, "it was really Asumali who started the quarrel. He likes to tease, but Mangoma is a good hunter and should not be treated like a youth. If these two are fighting, the hunt will be spoiled tomorrow and the camp will be hungry."

Just then Asumali joined us at the fire. Apparently he was often the cause of camp disagreements, and I don't think he was too surprised to find himself being blamed by the group for the row with Mangoma. He knew he was being blamed, because everyone around the fire ignored him. This was his punishment and he accepted it by walking off alone into the forest. Arumbu, a renowned hunter who had killed several elephants, sent his wife, Mateso, to Mangoma's hut with a choice piece of smoked venison, which was being kept for bartering with the local Lese villagers. Everybody agreed this was fair and a good thing to do. Not long afterward Mangoma joined us at the fire wearing a new cloth and quietly accepted his turn with the pipe that was being passed around. The subject of conversation turned to the hunting plans for the next day, and when Asumali returned to the fire, he was glad to find himself welcome to participate. The row was over and the well-being of the band was no longer jeopardized.

There were two basenji dogs in camp, and it was decided that the more active hunters would go with these in the morning to an area where fresh signs of antelope had been seen. I was becoming quite fit from daily walks through the forest, and Arumbu, whose opinion was most respected among the hunters, agreed to take me along.

It rained that night, but the forest was sunny and warm the next morning. After breakfast the dogs became excited when wooden bells were tied around their necks. Although they can whine loudly, basenjis can't bark, and the bells are to let the hunters know where they are when in pursuit of a wounded animal. I came to like these dogs, both of which had the alert manner and curled tail of the true basenji. They were obviously delighted when we finally left the camp with them. Many basenjis used by Efe hunters are technically owned by villagers who hope to receive meat occasionally for their ownership of the dogs.

I was a little worried to see the younger hunters run off and disappear into the forest ahead of us, but when we neared the place where the animals were supposed to be hiding, the dogs were restrained, and everybody came together again and maintained silence. Each hunter had a bow and a quiver full of arrows, even the boys. Arumbu, who owned one of the dogs, also carried a spear. He took the middle path with two boys, and I went with them. The remaining hunters split into two lines and disappeared among the trees to surround the thicket ahead of us. The plan was for us in the middle to act as beaters and drive the game out of the undergrowth into the arrows of the waiting hunters. It was a method that left much to chance, especially as there were not enough archers to form a complete circle around the beaters and dogs. Nothing was killed on the first two drives except a mongoose. But on the third try in a different place a young mboloko antelope was killed with a single metal-tipped arrow through the heart.

The mongoose hanging from Ubufu's belt and the little antelope were not much to eat for an entire Mbuti band, and so we kept trying. On the fourth attempt, the dogs flushed a plump red duiker antelope, and with their wooden bells rattling loudly, they chased it directly toward Sukali, who hit it with an arrow. But it was not a severe wound and when Sukali pounced on the animal, it gored him viciously in the groin with one of its sharp little horns. Sukali's anguished yells quickly brought his friends, but by then the antelope was gone. The younger hunters quickly followed the sound of the bells as the dogs took up the chase, but the scent was lost in a swampy area.

In the weeks I had been at Camp Tupi, my willingness to provide whatever medical assistance I could to those who needed it had made me into a kind of amateur Dr. Schweitzer. I had no formal medical training but had grown up in a family that had produced four physicians from the one household. For years some of my closest friends were medical students and young doctors in residence. Out of curiosity and to pass the time during those years, there were countless times when I accepted the invitation to don a white coat and attend clinics, operations, births, and autopsies. They were a crazy group, those medical-student friends of my youth, but something of their underlying dedication rubbed off on me which I often later put to good use in situations where I unwillingly found myself the only person with any medical knowledge at all.

Fortunately for Sukali, his wound was relatively superficial. The antelope's horn had penetrated the skin but missed the femoral artery. There was not much bleeding, and as we were so few, he gamely limped on to continue with the hunt.

Our luck began to change dramatically an hour later when Ubufu spotted a giant forest hog disappearing into a clump of undergrowth. He had the good sense to quickly retreat and inform Arumbu, the band's best hunter and the only one armed with a spear. Speed was important if the hunters were to surround the animal before it scented us, or heard the dogs, which sometimes made yelping sounds.

Each dog was held back until Arumbu and three other hunters had circled to the far side of where the animal was hiding. Only then were the dogs released into the undergrowth, with the remaining hunters following close behind.

Arumbu had positioned himself well, for the giant hog ran directly toward him. When it swerved at the last moment, he flung his broad-bladed spear with all his considerable strength, and it pierced the massive animal through the chest. It continued running, blood pouring from its mouth, but the dogs quickly caught up with it, and the beast turned to fight, the spear still buried deep in its side. It was an old solitary boar, weighing about two hundred pounds, and with its long, upward curving tusks, it made a formidable picture. But the spear must have severed a major artery, for the unfortunate beast soon collapsed and died, to the disappointment of the dogs, which were working themselves up to a good fight.

The hunters were ecstatic. This giant forest hog, covered in long, glistening black hair, contained as much meat as perhaps eight mboloko antelope. Within minutes its carcass was being cut up into loads that each man would carry back to camp. Yet even before we reached Camp Tupi, the women who had returned from their gathering knew all about our success from the hunters' elbow clapping and shouts, which traveled great distances through the forest ahead of them.

The elbow clapping, as I called it, was done by cupping an elbow against the chest and slapping it forcefully with the other hand. This produced a noise like a loud hand clap, and by slapping it in different ways the returning hunters could send advance information to the camp on what they killed.

That evening there was continuous dancing and singing, and even the dogs were well fed from the scraps that, because of the abundance of food, were more meaty than usual. As entertainment, the goring of Sukali was reenacted many times, with two hunters playing the roles of Sukali and the antelope that attacked him. Even the quarrelsome Asumali was in a lighthearted mood, playing the part of the giant forest hog in a reenactment of the hunt. Mangoma played the part of Arumbu, repeatedly thrusting a makeshift spear to within an inch of Asumali's side. Apparently they were good friends once again. Later in the evening I saw Sukali dancing enthusiastically around the fire, his wound forgotten.

To the Mbuti, an excess of meat means wealth. To have it makes them independent of the need to work. Indeed, during the brief period of their wealth most Mbuti blatantly spend their time in the pursuit of pleasure, just as more permanently wealthy people do elsewhere. The festive mood of that evening continued into the next day and nobody went hunting. Most huts had meat being smoke-dried on wooden platforms over the family hearths. Although there were baskets of mushrooms, roots, and fruits left over from the previous day's gathering, two of the women took some of the meat in baskets and set out on the six-hour walk to the village of their "patrons" to barter it for bananas, palm oil, and cassava. This was an event that would occur every few days, and even more often during my stay. For I would provide money in addition to the meat (of which there was not always a surplus). I hoped that word of my presence would not bring inquisitive villagers to look me over.

What do the Mbuti do when they don't have to hunt and gather? Plenty. But first there are always the routine chores that make a camp function: collecting firewood, fetching water, cooking the morning meal, and tending the children. Yet with the sheer exuberance and joy of living that I have seen only among the Mbuti, there were also spontaneous dances and singing, adding to the sounds of a happy camp. At the forest's edge, laughing children were swinging from a hanging vine a hundred feet long while nearby a few girls were acrobatically skipping rope, using a length of liana with the greatest dexterity. And always there was the steady *tap-tap* of someone hammering a piece of bark.

The making of bark cloth is one of the truly satisfying, creative tasks for the Mbuti, both male and female. First cutting a section of bark from a suitable tree, a hunter peels off the softer inner layer. Then he will pound this on a log into a fibrous cloth. His choice of tree, the initial cut, and the way he pounds it will dictate the final shape, quality, and size of the piece.

Traditionally the women will then paint on the designs, using a black vegetable dye, although they sometimes add a red dye if a piece is to be particularly admired. The paintings are usually geometric in concept, yet I have sometimes seen interesting variations, including a piece resembling a spotted leopard skin. A woman can paint whatever she likes and does not have to conform to any tribal or traditional pattern. An artist's materials cost nothing, and time in the Ituri is not measured in dollars.

I strolled over to where Mangoma's daughter was sitting on a mat of mongongo leaves. Alita was the smallest Mbuti Pygmy girl I had ever seen, being just under four feet tall. She might have been mistaken for a child except for her fully formed, firm young breasts, of which she was very proud and which she painted almost every day. Her face was quite beautiful, with large, lustrous eyes and a ready, flirtatious smile that could melt the heart of any man. Her skin was light brown, turning to gold in the sunlight. What she lacked in stature she made up in spirit, and she often led the other girls and women in singing and dancing. Stretched across her bare thighs was a piece of bark cloth that she had been painting in her spare time for several days. She was singing quietly to herself and seemed especially happy, perhaps because the day had come when she could wear her new cloth when she danced for all to see and admire. She looked up with a mischievous smile when I sat down on a log beside her. Like others in the camp, she had come to accept my habit of wandering around asking questions and writing notes. "Do you want to buy this nice cloth?" she asked jokingly, holding it up for me to see.

I took it from her and pulled it up between my legs in Mbuti fashion. "It's too small for me," I said, pretending disappointment.

"Or maybe you're too big for it." She giggled and snatched it back.

Sukali had joined us a few minutes earlier and laughed when I tried on the bark cloth. "Did you know," he said, "that Alita cannot marry anybody in Camp Tupi because everybody here is her brother or cousin? Maybe if you kill an antelope and give it to her father, Alita can be your wife. And then," he added brightly, "you will have somebody to cook for you and fix your hut when it leaks."

I had come to like Sukali, and he in turn looked on me as his special friend because he was the one who had brought me to Camp Tupi. In addition, we had learned to appreciate each other's sense of humor.

"How could she cook for me?" I asked. "She's too small even to lift a cooking pot off the fire."

Sukali pondered for a moment before slapping his thigh. "You can give her a small cooking pot," he exclaimed, and ran off laughing when Alita flipped some paint at his face. "Remember," he shouted, "you're the only man at Camp Tupi who can sleep with her. Anybody else will be accused of incest!"

There was much laughing from those who heard. Her father, Mangoma, laughed loudest of all.

If Alita was the smallest unmarried girl in camp, her brother Ubufu, who sat nearby making arrows, was the most unusual looking. Although he had nearly the same amount of body hair as the average adult male Mbuti, this young hunter had fully developed, well-formed breasts of which many women would be proud. The condition called gynecomastia exists to some degree in many Mbuti, although usually only to the extent of their excessively developed nipples. When I first met Ubufu, I was momentarily confused, not knowing if I was meeting a male or female person, especially since either would be unclothed above the waist. The amount and location of body hair was not necessarily an indication of gender either, as there was a young married woman in camp who had hair growing on her chest between her breasts. At a distance only the bow and arrows Ubufu sometimes carried readily identified him as a hunter, especially as men and women cut their head hair in the same style.

Shouts of "Snake! Snake!" at the edge of camp quickly brought a crowd to where Mazero was dramatically pointing to beneath a rotting log. On the ground nearby lay the water pot she had dropped when the snake had startled her. Only the sudden hiss at her feet, she told everybody, had saved her life. She was probably correct, for when her husband, Mokono, killed the snake with a spear, I was able to positively identify it as a large horned viper, one of the deadliest snakes in all Africa.

The Mbuti, and especially the Efe, will eat snakes, even the horned viper. But with so much other meat presently available in camp, Mokono chopped off the snake's head, slit open its thick body, and tossed it to one of the dogs.

Somehow the incident seemed to remind those in camp about their various medical ailments, for shortly afterward I treated a woman with a splinter of wood buried deep in her foot, followed by a boy with a painful tropical ulcer on his lower leg. I handed out aspirin to several people for headaches and other aches and pains.

If the camp had a patriarch, it was Ndima, the oldest man in the band and the father of Arumbu. He approached me feebly every day with complaints of body aches, and I routinely gave him two aspirin each time he came. One man, a visitor from another camp, had a genuine case of malaria, and I gave him something more appropriate. He had come with a woman who had carried with her a two-year-old boy who had a bad case of yaws. The disease had eaten away part of one buttock and part of his scrotum, and the poor little fellow was crying pitifully. A single injection of penicillin would have effected a cure, but I had none, nor the refrigeration to keep it viable if I had. I sadly watched the mother carry the suffering child away on the long walk back to their camp, and for the hundredth time I swore that one day if I could afford it I would come back into the forest with the facilities to treat such curable diseases. But such moments of despair were rare, if only because the optimistic and happy outlook of the Mbuti did not long allow anything to interrupt the flow of life in the camp.

Arumbu's pregnant wife Mateso was obviously ready to deliver any day now. When she had previously come to me for medicine, I jokingly told her that I thought she was going to have twins. It was a remark I immediately regretted, as twins are not welcome among the Mbuti. Because a woman must walk long distances each day through the forest, the burden of having to carry an extra baby on the breast would be too much to bear. And so it is said that a Mbuti mother smothers a twin soon after birth. Certainly I have never seen twins among the Mbuti.

When Mateso had first come for medicine, she brought her daughter, Deta, a charming little girl of about seven to whom I gave a half-bar of candy in its original colorful wrapper. It was no more than a mouthful, but Mateso immediately took possession of it, and all little Deta received was a tiny fragment the size of a pea, just enough for her to experience the taste. Two days later I saw Mateso taking the same piece of candy from where she had hidden it in the roof of her hut. She broke off another tiny piece and gave it to Teketeke, the little daughter of Mokono and Mazero. Then the half-bar of candy was carefully wrapped up again and returned to its place high among the leaves of her hut. Its ten cents' worth was apparently going to last for several days and be shared among many people.

Most of the hunters sat around the central fire, passing around a pipe filled with a blend of dried tobacco leaves and bangi. The tobacco I had bought in a roadside store, and the bangi had been acquired from a Lese villager. Although bangi is illegal in

Zaire, it is an item commonly bartered by the village farmers in exchange for meat. Both men and women among the Mbuti like to smoke it. If one wants to insure a welcome in an Mbuti hunting camp, one arrives with a quantity of bangi discreetly packed with his other goods.

As we sat in the circle, Sukali came and asked if I wanted to see the spring where the purest water flowed. We had talked about it previously but had never taken the time to go there. With nothing much happening in the camp at the moment, it seemed an ideal opportunity, and so I collected my water bottle and we set off together into the forest. Sukali seemed to be in a purposeful mood. "Do you like Alita?" he unexpectedly asked over his shoulder as I followed him along the narrow track.

"She's a very beautiful girl," I answered. "Of course I like her." I was curious to know why he should ask, but we walked for another minute before Sukali spoke again.

"You know because she is a museka she can sleep with anybody she likes until she becomes married," he said.

"Yes, I know," I told him, well aware of the sexual freedom that the Mbuti enjoy. "But why are you telling me this? You already have a wife, Ndasu, who is also a beautiful girl."

Sukali shurgged. "Ndasu is not completely my wife. She's still a museka just like Alita."

"What do you mean?" I asked. "Surely she's your wife. You both sleep in the same hut together every night."

"Yes, but we're not really married until we have a child, a child who lives long enough to be given the name of its grandfather or grandmother," Sukali said. "So I can sleep with any girl I like, even Alita," he boasted. I knew that the young unmarried Mbuti practice *arobo*, or free love, which is why Sukali so gleefully claimed he was not *completely* married.

"But Alita is your cousin. She's from your own clan. Surely the Mbuti don't allow such incest," I jested.

"Of course," Sukali laughed, "but I have slept many times with every girl in Camp Tupi, and they're *all* my cousins!"

"What happens if you make a girl have a baby?" I asked.

"The girls learn ways from their mothers not to have babies before they are married," Sukali said.

"What kind of ways?" I asked, wondering if I had stumbled across a natural form of birth control. Sukali grinned at me over his shoulder.

"Only girls know about such things. Ask Alita tonight after the dancing."

"Tonight?" I asked. "Why tonight?" Sukali didn't bother to look around again.

"You'll see," he said mysteriously. "Tonight after the dancing."

We had walked for about ten minutes when Sukali motioned for me to be quiet. Ahead of us I could hear the sound of girls' voices. "We've come to the place of clean water, the spring I told you about," Sukali whispered. "This is where the girls are." He was walking quickly now, and I struggled to keep up.

"The girls?" I asked. "What girls?" He grinned, obviously enjoying the private joke.

"You'll see," he whispered.

In a moment we reached a rocky outcrop at the edge of which was a natural pool fed by a little waterfall. Through a wall of hanging vines we could see Alita and Ndasu. Both had hung their belts and bark cloths on a bush and were washing themselves in the sparkling water. "You knew they were here, didn't you?" I whispered accusingly to Sukali. His reply was to suddenly jump up with a fearsome yell and charge into the water, tearing off his bark cloth as he ran. He grabbed Alita and playfully pretended to copulate with her until he let himself be pulled away by a laughing Ndasu.

To either stay where I was or to walk back the way I came would make me appear rather silly. So I followed Sukali at least to the water's edge. When I appeared, both girls giggled and sat down in the shallow water to hide their nakedness. "Come in!" Sukali shouted, gleefully splashing water all about him. "We'll help them wash off the old paint so that they can put on beautiful new paint for the dancing!"

I decided to be a gentleman—or its equivalent in the Ituri forest—and went to trace the source of the little waterfall. I found it only a few yards away, a natural spring gurgling out from between two great slabs of rock. I made a cup from a mongongo leaf and drank some of the water. It was cool and entirely refreshing and decidedly preferable to the taste of water boiled over a smoky fire. I drank all I could before filling my water bottle. Just then I heard Sukali shouting, and I looked back to see him and Ndasu snatch up their bark cloths and belts and quickly run off together into the forest. I was flattered that Sukali should treat me like a fellow hunter of his own age group, but I would have preferred a more impersonal introduction to the mores of Mbuti free love. On the other hand, I was in the forest as a participant observer, and this moment seemed an inappropriate one to arbitrarily decide to be an observer only.

I picked up Alita's cloth and belt and walked around to where she sat on the edge of a rock with her legs dangling in the water. Now she seemed quite unconcerned with her nakedness and indeed appeared to be enjoying the situation as she reclined sensuously against the rock behind her and watched me approach with her mischievous smile. She made a picture that I will never forget.

Alita was proud of her firm young body, which had just recently flowered into womanhood. She would never own anything, yet this was her forest, and this was her special bathing place, which even King Croesus with all his wealth could not have duplicated. She had played naked in pools like this as a child, just as innocently as she played now. She had never learned to think of the human body or any of its functions as shameful and could not conceive of anyone else doing so.

To Alita this pool among the rocks and trees was where she happened to be today. Yesterday was past and gone forever. In the forest where death comes early, the uncertain tomorrows of her life could come and go all too quickly. Life was precious and too brief to waste the moment that was now.

An Mbuti woman passes through the stages of her life with regrettable brevity. From the age of about six—if she survives infancy—she is already caring for younger children and carrying bundles of firewood as heavy as herself. In the fleeting period between reaching puberty and becoming a married woman—a mere year or so—a girl joins the young unmarried hunters in the daily—and nightly—pursuit of sexual pleasures, for such is the Mbuti's way of selecting permanent mates for married life. In the sexual activities between both the married and unmarried Mbuti I have known, the two most effectively recognized taboos are incest between a brother and sister and homosexuality. Sexually intimate friendships between cousins are common, and indeed almost expected by individuals as a social right. Yet while cousins may develop and enjoy their sexual skills with each other, Mbuti society prohibits their marrying.

By the age of twenty, an Mbuti woman will ideally have had several children and can already appear middle-aged. By the time she is twenty-five, she will, in her bare feet, have walked a distance equal to about the circumference of the earth, carrying loads, and often a nursing infant, through rain, mud, and humidity that would make a hardened combat soldier weary. Although probably infected with parasitic worms, malaria, and unfriendly amoebas, she will, in common with the average Mbuti hunter who walks comparable distances, never see a doctor from the day she is born until she dies.

Alita now took her cloth and belt and began to put them on with unhurried movements. "Are you going to bathe too?" she asked me playfully, looking up with her enchanting, mischievous eyes. I answered with another question.

"Why didn't you run off with Sukali and Ndasu?" She finished tying the knot in her belt.

"Because," she said teasingly, "you could not find your way back to Camp Tupi alone."

She was right, of course. I probably couldn't.

I was beginning to feel that I had lost command of the situation to this tiny girl-woman, this miniature Venus who had risen lovely and flowerlike from the spring with drops of water glistening on the petals of her golden body. I thought wryly of my options and obligations as dictated by the artificial ethics of my alien culture. But if I ignored Alita and walked away, not only would I risk being hopelessly lost, I would also insult her personally. And I would have thrown Sukali into near terminal despair in his efforts to make me think as an Mbuti. "Let's go and find the others," I said, and we set off together in the direction they had gone.

A few minutes later we found Sukali and Ndasu enthusiastically copulating on the mossy bank of a stream. They took little notice of us when we almost stumbled over their entwined bodies which, for the anthropological record and the furthering of science, were not in the missionary position. We said "Karibu" (Hello) and kept on walking, which, under the circumstances, is the polite thing to do in Mbuti society, just as it would be elsewhere.

Just before dusk that day the powerfully built young hunter Mapoli wiped his greasy hands on his hairy legs and rose from a meal of giant forest hog. He belched noisily and wandered over to the single drum of Camp Tupi and tapped it sensitively to test the tautness of its skin. Apparently dissatisfied, he carried it over to the communal fire and held it close to the flames to shrink the skin tighter. It took only a minute before he carried it back to the drumming place and began to play.

Mapoli's mastery of the instrument made him undoubtedly the best drummer in Camp Tupi, and perhaps in all the forest, they said. His opening staccato passage thundered dramatically through the camp and far beyond into the forest. It was a message that no Mbuti could resist, a signal that said, "Come to the dance!" The message ended, and with his bare left hand and a stick in the other, Mapoli began to beat a forceful rhythm that soon brought all the Mbuti to their feet, even Ndima, the camp patriarch, and Arumbu's pregnant wife, Mateso.

Before long the men and women had formed two separate circles around the fire, both dancing in a counterclockwise direction, with the women on the outside. Someone stacked fresh wood on the fire, and its flames leaped higher to light the faces of the dancers as day faded into the sudden tropical night. Everybody joined in the singing, and gradually the mood grew more abandoned. The men's faces showed the grimaces and facial contortions for which they are known, and trickles of sweat began to appear. As they danced, some played bamboo flutes, ancient instruments rarely seen today. Sukali pranced his way past where I sat on my three-stick chair. As decoration, he wore the skin of a red colobus monkey dangling from his waist. Other men and women wore clusters of fresh green leaves hanging from the same place.

When each dance ended, another would begin with greater excitement as Mapoli's hypnotic music throbbed into the night. In the high humidity of the rain forest, his entire body was bathed in sweat as he played and played until both he and the dancers reached a kind of frenzy together. He produced a complex rhythm by alternately hitting his stick against the top of the drum and its wooden side while beating the skin with his left hand. His performance was superb, and the people loved it as they moved in precise synchronization with his every nuance and flick of the wrist. He was the maestro and the dancers were his responsive orchestra. They sang and danced what his drum told them to sing and dance, and rested only when he rested.

I looked up to see Alita and her friend Maguti join the dancers. In a moment they had found the step and were singing in unison with the others. They circled past me every minute, with the buxom Maguti supporting her bouncing breasts with her arm. Both girls had painted each other's body almost all over. I wondered if Alita would glance in my direction with her mischievous smile, but both she and Maguti kept their heads high and their expressions aloof. Their fathers, Mangoma and Asumali, were dancing in the inner circle, their faces glistening with sweat, their voices hoarse from bangi and singing. Beside them was Arumbu, the elephant hunter. He had danced every dance and sung every song with intense feeling. Tomorrow he would be his usual quiet self and appear to be almost a different person. His wife Mateso had bravely joined the dancing at first but soon left, supporting her swollen abdomen in her hands.

The dance might well have lasted halfway through the night except for the rainstorm that came our way. As its thunder came closer, the people one by one began to move their fires and extra firewood into their huts. Sukali came to tell me that this was being done for me, and I was grateful because nobody can move fire and magically make it burn as well as an Mbuti. I was one of those who decided to stay for one more dance but soon regretted it when the rain began with a deafening thunderclap and a sudden deluge that quickly soaked me to the skin. Somebody grabbed the drum and we all stumbled through the darkness to our huts.

For an Mbuti to get wet means very little, for he can hang his diminutive bark cloth from the lightest sapling in his hut. For me to get wet was more of a problem, for there would be little space in the Mbuti hut to dry my sodden clothes. In the Ituri rain forest, mold begins to grow on damp clothes overnight, and there is even one kind of fungus that grows on the human body, its roots penetrating the skin.

I crawled through the little entrance of my hut and was grateful for the fire that Sukali had arranged. The rain was extremely heavy and an Mbuti hut can be a chilly place when the forest is wet. I hung up my wet clothes as best I could and checked the fire, which seemed to have the habit of dying when I wasn't looking. On the far side of my tiny dwelling, a steady drip began, which I decided to ignore. Shivering in the suddenly damp, cold air, I pulled my single blanket around me and sat for a while, watching the firelight falling on the curtain of rain at the open doorway. It was one of those times when I had to ask myself what on earth was I doing there.

Unless one is born an Mbuti, a temporary, fragile, doorless shelter of sticks and leaves built without a floor directly on perpetually damp ground does little to reinforce one's sense of comfort or security, even on a bright, sunny day. There is no furniture unless one counts the incredibly uncomfortable bed some Mbuti use, which is made of a couple of bare tree branches lying horizontally on the ground. There are no bathroom facilities, no running water, no windows, no artificial light. To stand up, even an Mbuti Pygmy must first crawl outside. The only toilet is the great outdoors. The nearest road may be a six hours' walk away, and the nearest major city many days' journey beyond that. Except for a missionary hospital outside the forest at Nyakunde, the nearest medical help for a serious illness may be in Europe or South Africa. To spend the night alone, with a seemingly endless, torrential downpour battering relentlessly on a few sticks and leaves above one's head, is not for the nervous traveler who complains to the hotel manager about a leaking water tap.

Just when I was beginning to think that I was cut off from every other human being on earth, I saw a pair of muddy feet appear through the rain, and in a moment Alita ducked inside to sit breathlessly beside me. It was the second time that day that I had seen her soaking wet.

"Habari yako?" I greeted her. "Njema," she replied softly. "Na wewe?"

"I'm very well, thank you," I said. "Unataka kukaa hapa— do you want to stay here?" I asked her gently.

"Yes," she smiled. "Nataka kulala ndani ya nyumba yako— I want to sleep in your hut."

During the lengthy rain that night, I asked Alita many questions. I also found out the correct thing to do with her family, who were well aware of where she was spending the night. When she left at dawn, I gave her a stainless-steel hunting knife for her father, which I had brought from nine thousand miles away.

Apparently Mangoma was well pleased, for in the following weeks he loaned the knife around for a day at a time to each of his hunter friends. And for the rest of my stay with the band, my cooking and housekeeping problems were over at last, for Alita adopted me, and my fire never went out again.

# 6

## The Monkey Hunter

Each day the men took their bows and arrows and went hunting, sometimes alone. At other times they went in a group with the dogs. Ndeke was an older hunter who had reached an age when he no longer hunted with the group. This was not considered antisocial by the other men. Indeed, it was a tradition that old hunters would leave the more strenuous forms of hunting to the younger men and hunt alone. His weapon was a bow with which he used both poisoned and nonpoisoned arrows, depending on the quarry. He had once killed an elephant with a spear, but that was a long time ago.

I liked Ndeke, as did everybody else in camp. He was not only the best storyteller around, but also the unofficial historian of those he considered the People, the Bambuti. I had seen him leaving camp early most mornings, often to return in the afternoon with a monkey. Once I saw him come back with a small antelope. When I first asked Ndeke if I could accompany him into the forest, he took so long to reply that it seemed he hadn't heard me. He was making a new bow at the time, a task he approached with the quiet satisfaction of a craftsman. I waited while he whittled another delicate shaving from the almost completed weapon and watched while he squinted along its length to check the accuracy of his work. When he spoke, it was not to answer my question.

"In the place you come from," he asked, "do you eat nyama?" (*Nyama* means wild animal or—in this context—meat.) "Yes," I said. "My people eat meat almost every day."

"What kind of meat?" Ndeke asked. "Mboloko? Elephant?"

"No," I said. "We eat animals that are not wild, the way the Lese keep chickens and goats near their huts and eat them when they want to."

"These animals you kill, can they be found here in the forest?" Ndeke asked.

"We eat fish just like the fish here in the rivers of the forest—" I began.

"But what kind of nyama?" Ndeke insisted.

"We eat cattle," I told him, "and pigs and chickens like the ones they have on the farms at Bunia [an elevated farming area outside the forest]." Ndeke whittled a little more from his new bow.

"How do you kill these animals?" he asked carefully. I thought about it for a moment and realized that the killing of domesticated animals was not a subject with which I was particularly familiar. I knew how they killed cattle in the slaughterhouse or abattoir, but how did they finally slaughter the hardworking chickens after they had laid all those eggs?

"They kill the cattle with a kind of gun," I said, "and I think they kill the chickens with a knife."

Ndeke held up his battered old bow and asked, "If I went to your country, would I see any people with this?" I realized he probably wasn't serious because he knew that even among the Lese villagers one does not generally see anyone except an Mbuti with a bow and a quiver of arrows slung over his shoulder. I shook my head.

"No," I told him truthfully, wondering what was coming next.

"Here," he said, handing me his old bow and a single arrow. "The tree over there is an elephant. Kill it!"

I took his trusty old weapon and carefully put the reed arrow in the firing position—it was obvious he wasn't about to waste a precious metal-tipped arrow on me—and aimed at the giant tree just fifteen paces away. The arrow barely hit the tree and glanced off in a sad trajectory to the ground. "But you kill elephants with a spear, not an arrow," I said as I handed back the bow.

Ndeke's manner was as reproving as it was gently forgiving. "If the tree was a monkey or a bird, you would be hungry tonight!"

When Ndeke left for the forest the next day, I went with him. I knew that he primarily intended to hunt monkeys because his quiver contained mostly all-wooden arrows treated with poison, and poisoned arrows are rarely used on anything but monkeys. He also carried a few metal-tipped arrows in case there was an opportunity to shoot an antelope or other larger animal such as a chevrotain or bush pig.

For the Mbuti, monkey hunting is usually a solitary affair, with a single hunter walking quietly through the forest until he hears a troop of monkeys. If they are high in the trees, his little bow is ineffective, so he stalks them until one or all of the monkeys come halfway down the trees to feed. Ndeke knew that many monkeys do this in the morning and the late afternoon.

Monkeys have keen eyesight, so when we later heard monkeys chattering somewhere ahead, I was glad that my clothes were of a neutral khaki color. Ndeke removed the protective covering of leaves he had wrapped around the poisoned tips of the arrows and glanced at me as he fitted an arrow to his bow. He must have thought, as I did, that his chances of success were lessened by my presence. Monkeys are curious, but also very cautious.

The morning mists still lingered and the moisture-laden air was almost palpable as I followed Ndeke on his stalk. We both finally crouched beneath our quarry, a troop of blue monkeys. They were scattered high among the tall trees, leaping playfully from branch to branch and apparently unaware or uncaring of our presence. While it would have been easy to shoot one with a rifle, they were out of range of Ndeke's arrows unless they came down to the lower branches.

Ndeke had been hunting monkeys all his life, and to patiently wait or to stalk perhaps just one or two steps in five minutes was merely part of his daily work. Once in view of the monkeys, his movements became those of a chameleon, so that unless one stared at him constantly, he did not seem to move at all. On the final stalk he held his bow constantly aimed upward, ready to shoot in an instant without any movement except from his fingers releasing the deadly arrow.

I had respectfully fallen behind, and from a distance I watched the monkeys above Ndeke gradually come lower in the trees. Finally, one fine specimen leaped to a branch within range and found itself looking down the shaft of Ndeke's poisoned arrow. Almost at the moment it landed, I heard the twang of the bow-string and the monkey was hit. It screamed and quickly retreated well out of range to the highest branches. But it was doomed to die even without a second shot. I joined Ndeke and together we followed the troop as they fled through the treetops above us.

The poison Ndeke used is made by the Mbuti from the sap of a forest vine, of the genus *Strophanthus*. Ironically, yet another kind of vine provides them with a medicine they apply directly to open wounds to heal them more quickly. In his writings Stanley gave the impression that the Mbuti Pygmies' poison could kill almost immediately. But this is apparently not so. On each occasion I have seen a monkey hit with a poisoned arrow, there was a delay of up to an hour before the animal fell out of the trees. Meanwhile, it easily scampered off with the troop through the trees, and only the extremely skilled efforts of the hunter following below made it possible for us to be there when the monkey finally died. It is said that the "poison" paralyzes rather than poisons the victim.

That day we followed the monkeys until at last Ndeke spotted the wounded one beginning to lag behind the others. In moments the troop was gone, leaving their dying companion alone high up in a tall tree. It glanced down at us and attempted to leap to another tree. But in its weakened or semiparalyzed condition it fell short and thudded to the ground near where we stood.

Ndeke and I went into the forest together quite often after that first day. Sometimes he did not succeed in killing anything except a squirrel or a bird, and once the only thing he brought back was a live tortoise, which was killed and eaten a few days later when there was not much meat in camp. Yet, even if Ndeke failed to bring back a worthwhile kill, he would as often return with a collection of berries, nuts, or insect larvae. Twice he brought back my favorite forest food, which he shared with me. A kind of fungus locally called *malenge,* it grows only inside termite hills where the termites cultivate it as food on the fecal wood and leaves that have passed through their own alimentary canals. I was so impressed with the exotic quality of this rare delicacy that I had included a sequence on it in my film on the Mbuti, which I made years earlier. At that time I compared its taste to that of mushrooms, but considered it even better.

Ndeke was always on the lookout for trees from which ripe fruit or seeds were falling, for antelopes like to eat such food. When he found such a place near recent antelope tracks, we would both crouch down while he imitated the sound of a baby antelope frantically calling its mother. The hope was that a mother would come bounding straight into the range of the hunter's arrow. I had seen an old hunter doing this in Zambia, using a wooden whistle he had made to call gray duiker antelope. Instead, the Mbuti blow through their hands to the same effect. It doesn't always work, and Ndeke tried it for several days before we even saw an antelope. It was a female mboloko and it came running into our clearing apparently believing the call was real. Ndeke's iron-tipped arrow pierced the animal's throat and it died before it could run more than fifty paces.

Once we were at the edge of a rare forest clearing stalking some monkeys when suddenly they all panicked. A large eagle was swooping at great speed toward one of the troop feeding precariously on the outer end of a high branch. The giant bird struck hard with talons that must have been enormous, for it lifted its helpless but still struggling victim clear of the tree and

Basenji dog with wooden bell attached to neck.

Archer.

Hunter making poison for arrows.

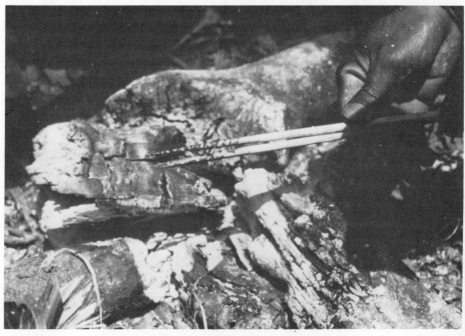

Drying poison over fire on tips of arrows.

Archer with blue duiker he has shot.
The arrows he carries have poisoned tips covered with leaves to protect
him from accidental cut.

Hunter with sondo (red forest duiker) antelope he killed with arrow.

Dividing meat of antelope.

Woman receives share of meat.

Hunter and wife at net with mboloko antelope (blue forest duiker) they have speared.

Older hunter with monkey he has killed.

Villagers buying meat from mbuti Pygmies.

flew off. I had heard that this bird kills its larger prey by dropping it to the ground from a great height, and I wondered how far it would have to fly before it found a suitable clearing between the trees.

Even Ndeke was excited and didn't seem to care that his stalk had been spoiled. Indeed, I believe he was envious of this winged hunter of the forest that had powers he did not himself possess. "Since I was a child," he told me, "I have seen the big bird kill like this only twice." Then he asked thoughtfully, "You have not seen it before now, have you?"

I had known of the great bird's existence—it is commonly known as the "monkey-killing eagle"—but I had never before seen it with my own eyes. In fact, I must have been more impressed than Ndeke. "No," I said. "I have never seen it before now, and I thank you because now I have seen it." Indeed, only if a pteranodon had carried off the simian creature would I have been more impressed.

Not long after the eagle had spoiled our first stalk, we encountered another troop of monkeys. They were red colobuses, a favorite of the Mbuti hunters, who like to peel off their tail skins intact and pull them over the wood of their bows as decoration—and as visible proof of their hunting skill. Ndeke succeeded in wounding one of these monkeys with a poisoned arrow, and we began to follow it in a direction away from Camp Tupi. I had not previously gone this far into the forest with Ndeke, and when he suddenly stopped, I thought that perhaps he was tired and had decided to abandon the chase.

Instead, he turned to me and said something most intriguing. "That monkey," he told me quietly, "it is leading us straight into the center of the world." He used the word *forest* in a context that meant the world, for to him the forest is the world. I was curious to see this place that no one had mentioned to me previously.

"What do you mean, the center of the forest?" I asked him. Ndeke looked at me as if doubting the wisdom of confiding in a Muzungu.

"Because," he said slowly, "it is the place where God lives."

Although the Mbuti in various areas have different names and descriptions for God, it seems that they all believe in a supernatural power which they closely associate with the forest itself. In the Ituri, as in many parts of Africa, the word *Mungu* has become a universal term for God, although each language group may continue to use its tribal word or words for a supreme god over all things.

"I would like to see this place where God lives," I said. "Can you take me there?"

Ndeke sat on a log and thought for a moment. "There is a great snake guarding that place," he warned, "and always the place is cold because there is no sun there."

It was doubtful that Ndeke had ever been influenced by missionaries, and I was fascinated by his story. "I would like to go there," I said again.

Ndeke seemed uncomfortable. "It is a dangerous place for a sick person or an old man to visit, because nearby there is a cave where *Tore* lives with the *Lodi*—the spirits of the dead. A sick or old person who sees Tore will die and become a Lodi. I am an old man and do not want to meet Tore."

"Have you seen the snake that guards the place where God lives?" I asked.

"No, I have not seen it," Ndeke said quietly. "But anyone can see it who goes there."

It was becoming late and I did not expect him to change his mind. Already I was planning to go with Sukali, assuming he knew the way there. "What do you call this place that is the center of the forest?" I asked.

"It is called Apalura," he said. "My grandfather took me there when I was a boy."

I had been compiling a list of Kilese-Efe words and I knew that *apalura* meant butterflies. It was a lovely name for the place where God lives.

"Do you remember your grandfather well?" I asked.

"Yes," Ndeke said reflectively. "I remember him as well as I remember my father. I was given his name, as many Mbuti children are given their grandparents' names." He was sitting on a log, gazing at something far away in the forest. The mention of his grandfather seemed to have put him in a nostalgic mood, and it was at moments like these that Ndeke liked to talk about his forest world.

"You have visited Apalura," I said. "Have you ever seen God?"

For a moment Ndeke was startled enough to turn and stare at me. Then he smiled in his gentle way and said, "When you see the forest, you see God."

It was my turn to be surprised. "You say that when I see the forest I see God. Is the forest God?"

For several moments an almost gnomelike Ndeke sat there, adorned only in the worn and faded bark cloth he had once made with his own hands from a piece of the forest. His gaze slowly wandered across the seemingly infinite trees among which he had been born and where he would die. "Without the forest," he finally said, "there is no God, and without God there is no forest."

"What happens," I asked, "when you cut down a tree to get honey, or gather mongongo leaves to cover your hut? Does it make God angry when you burn the wood of the forest for your fire?"

Ndeke reflected for several moments and reached out to touch the delicate moss growing from a nearby branch. "The first Mbuti was born in the forest," he said, "and all Bambuti have been born here ever since. The forest is our mother and father, and we are its children. The forest would not want us to be cold or hungry."

"Then the forest *is* God?" I asked. But Ndeke did not answer. "What does God look like," I asked, "the one you call Grandfather?"

Ndeke examined the arrows in his quiver as he answered. "He is an old man with a long white beard," he said simply.

Schebesta recorded such a story concerning an anthropomorphic deity he had heard of among the Efe. His informant said that an aged man whom the Mbuti called Grandfather was lord of the lightning and the rainbow. He lived in the heavens, and when he swung his beard to and fro, violent thunderstorms and rains descended upon the earth.

"Is God an Mbuti?" I asked, and waited as Ndeke seemed to weigh my question. "No," he answered finally. "God is not a man. No one knows what God is, but he is not a man."

"Then, who is the old man with the white beard whom you call Grandfather?"

"If God let us see him, that is what we would see," Ndeke told me quietly.

"Is Tore God?" I asked.

Ndeke shrugged. "Some people say Tore is God, but I do not think so. Tore is lord of the forest and of the dead. We ask him to drive away the rain and to guide our arrows so that we shall not be hungry. But he is not God."

"Have you seen God?" I asked again. Ndeke fitted an arrow to his bow and aimed it at an imaginary target among the trees. When he finally answered, there was a note of disapproval in his voice. "No," he said. "I have never seen God. No one can see God. Have you seen him?"

"No," I answered, "but perhaps we do not have the same god?" Ndeke was already shaking his head.

"We may call him by different names," he said, "but there is only one great God over everything, and we are all his children."

We sat silently for a while as we watched a flock of parrots fly noisily overhead. It was time to return to camp, but there was one more question I wanted to raise that perhaps had less to do with religion than mythology. "Do you know," I asked, "where the first Mbuti came from?"

Ndeke seemed more relaxed with such a question. As he was a storyteller, it was the kind of subject he liked to talk about around the camp fires. He paused only a moment to reflect. "A long time ago," he began, "there was only one man living in all the forest. His name was Ochiosa, and one day God sent a woman to him so that he would not be lonely. Ochiosa had never seen a woman before and so thought that she had been wounded in the place where he expected a man's penis to be.

Making some medicine from a vine of the forest, he put it in the wound and the woman later bore a son called Luembe, who was the first Mbuti." I took the story to mean that Luembe was born of the forest—that the forest was his biological father.

In the weeks to come, Ndeke and the old man Ndima told me other legends of how the first Mbuti arrived on earth, and each account was different from the first I had been told. In other parts of the forest, I knew, different Mbuti each had their own creation stories and each their own version of a supreme being and numerous lesser supernatural beings and spirits. Nine years earlier, I had photographed a tiny spirit house built outside an Mbuti camp, in which food offerings had been left for ancestors in imitation of the villagers' ancestor worship.

I could understand what the Reverend Paul Schebesta meant when he wrote, in the early 1930s, of Mbuti theology: "What I have said about their legends and songs also applies to the religion of the Pygmies: each forms his own ideas, mostly according to his own taste. The amount of material which I gathered about their attitude towards this life and the hereafter is so varied and extensive that it would require a small volume to itself." In describing the same subject, Colin Turnbull wrote in his book *Wayward Servants* (1965), "However . . . there is not only difference of opinion from one net-hunting band to the next, but even within any one band or any one family."

If the Mbuti do not have a sense of political unity, it is equally apparent that they do not have a unified religion. Perhaps they once did before they became segmented linguistically—and to some extent culturally—into three major language groups: Lese, Medje, and Bila (or Bira). Of these languages, only Bila is of Bantu origin, while the others are Sudanic, with a different root and structure. It is hardly surprising to find that not only do different Mbuti groups have different hunting methods, but that they have different religious conceptions as well. It is only surprising to find that despite the constant potential of ravages from alien cultures, the basic Mbuti way of life throughout the

Ituri forest should have remained as separate and intact as it apparently did.

If the Mbuti do not all have the same conception of God, they do generally believe that each person has a soul. The ancient religious belief that human beings consist of a mysterious compound of physical matter and intangible spirit runs as deeply among the Mbuti as in any other people. And like other people, they believe that the nonmaterial self survives the death of the physical body and brain.

The Efe Mbuti call this intangible spirit *megbe* and think of it as an invisible, vital force, or soul, that leaves the body and divides into several parts when a person dies. The eldest son traditionally places his lips over his dying father's mouth at the moment of death and inhales a part of his megbe as it escapes. Another part of the dead person's megbe enters the dead man's totem—usually an animal such as a chimpanzee or leopard—in which form the one who died will continue to exist in the forest.

Yet another part of the megbe becomes a spirit called a Lodi, who lives in another dimension in the forest with other Lodi. Such a spirit can show itself, but is usually invisible to people who have not died. So, even if the eldest son fails to inhale his father's megbe, or someone kills the totem chimpanzee or leopard, a dead man's megbe will survive to live forever as a Lodi and become one of the children of Tore, lord of the forest and of the dead.

# 7

ɣ

## Birth and Death

One morning I awakened in camp feeling grimy and itchy all over and decided to begin the day with a bath in the river. It had been raining during the night, but already slanted sunbeams were searching among the trees to dissipate the morning mist. As I approached the water with Alita, a multitude of unseen frogs greeted us with their guttural chorus, and somewhere on the other side of the river a troop of monkeys jabbered for a few moments and was gone. We found a secluded place downstream that was surrounded by ferns and moss-covered trees. It looked as if it had never been visited by human beings before.

Alita had brought a cooking pot used the previous evening, and I watched her clean it with a mixture of sand and water, remembering that soap is a commodity not normally found in an Mbuti camp. I had brought three pieces of soap with me when I came into the forest, but within hours Sukali had discovered them and triumphantly carried off a piece to share with his friends. By the next day, he was back asking for more. Apparently almost the entire camp had used the first piece to wash themselves and whatever clothes they had in the river.

Now everything was back to normal in Camp Tupi, with no soap of any kind available for anybody, including myself. Once it was known that I had soap—or for that matter anything that was useful or edible to an Mbuti—it would have been considered antisocial of me to selfishly hoard it instead of sharing. Essentially, this meant my giving away almost everything I had until there was nothing left to give except medicines.

When my own food supplies finally ran out, I began to eat whatever everybody else in camp ate and drank, with my hosts now providing the food from a supply that would not run out as long as the daily hunting and gathering were successful. At such a time, I was quite aware that the Mbuti could survive without me and my few imported luxuries, but I could not survive without the Mbuti.

But I am wandering from the subject of soap and my attempts to stay clean without it. While I enjoy living among nonliterate peoples whose lives are not ruled by order and cleanliness, there always comes a time when I feel that I at least need to have my hair and beard trimmed. Mbuti men and women both keep their hair relatively short, and the Afro hairstyle seen in America is not popular in Africa. As a Muzungu, I was different enough already without willingly assuming a long-haired, wild-Muzungu-of-Africa appearance. Meanwhile, my bathing in the river without soap was satisfying enough for the moment and my haircut could wait a little longer.

Among the Mbuti I have known, the men do not wash or bathe daily, even if there is a stream or river nearby. The women do so more regularly, perhaps because they must go to the river at least once a day to fetch water. Menstruating women bathe frequently, perhaps twice daily if it is not raining. Tampons are unknown, and a sanitary pad of raw bark cloth would presumably be both uncomfortable and impractical on the long daily walks, especially in the rain. Children are not weaned from the breast until they are about two years old, and mothers with infants slung against their bodies for many hours every day, and nursing during the night, also bathe frequently. Except for mongongo leaves, the Mbuti do not have waterproof materials, and diapers, even if available, would probably be unhealthy in the humid rain forest, where harmful bacteria and fungus spores are ever-present and waiting for a host.

The Mbuti are much more relaxed toward such a natural occurrence as menstruation than are the village people, who view it with fear and dread. When an Mbuti girl experiences her first period, she is already well aware of what it means and feels only pride and pleasure with her new status and sexually active role. It is also an occasion for happiness in the entire Mbuti band, for a child of the community has successfully reached womanhood, thus adding to the general well-being and continuity of the group as a whole. There are no taboos associated with sexual intercourse during menstruation other than an Mbuti's personal preference.

Among many tribal peoples in tropical Africa, however, including the Ituri villagers, menstruation is regarded with apprehension and outright fear. During this time, a woman is regarded as unclean and dangerous to those around her. Such an attitude is demonstrated when a woman ceases to cook for her husband during her menstruation, as to touch his food is thought to endanger his health or even his life. A sister or a friend's wife will cook for him instead. This widespread taboo is based on the assumption that menstruation is not necessarily a natural event, but may have resulted from witchcraft or sorcery, or even from improper activity by the woman herself.

I have seldom seen Mbuti with decayed teeth, even among the elderly. I do not know if this results from inherently hard tooth enamel or a natural, sugar-free diet, or a combination of both. Perhaps it's something in the natural toothbrush the Mbuti make by breaking off a slender branch from a local tree and using its frayed end to brush their teeth. I have tried it myself and the taste was bitter but refreshing.

That afternoon the weather was calm and sultry. The hunters had each gone into the forest alone and among them had brought back a variety of animals. These included two monkeys and also a python, which Arumbu had killed with his spear. With the additional mushrooms, grubs, and caterpillars the women had gathered, we would dine well that evening. Everybody was in a happy, contented mood, and some of the people were attending to the kind of activities the Mbuti enjoy on a rainless afternoon when the day's hunting and gathering have been successful.

Bakbara was a woman who lived alone. She had been married to a villager as a second wife and had provided him with several children. But when she grew old and unattractive, her village husband sent her back to the forest and kept the children in the village. Her nearest living Mbuti relatives were her brother Ndeke and his married daughters, who lived in neighboring camps. By extension, that made her a second cousin of Ndima, and therefore related to his son, Arumbu.

That day Bakbara was having her head shaved in the way that some old Mbuti, both men and women, adopt. Asumali's wife, Matuneo, was the barber, and her tool was a crude knife made by a village blacksmith. By constantly dipping her fingers in a pot of water, Matuneo kept her subject's hair wet as she cut and scraped laboriously until Bakbara's head was totally bare and shiny all over. Somehow the treatment gave Bakbara a rather distinguished and noble appearance, and since among the Mbuti, permanently exposed breasts of married or older women have no sexual connotation whatsoever, I believe that the shaving of Bakbara's head placed her in an asexual social niche reserved for both older men and women who have become equally valued and respected by the band. By the way, I don't think that Matuneo's skill with the knife—which did not include a single cut to Bakbara's scalp—was for the more practical purpose of removing head lice.

Not long afterward I found Bakbara lovingly painting decorative lines and other shapes with a black dye on the face and body of Sibaku's granddaughter, Deta. About seven, the little girl snuggled happily between Bakbara's legs, enjoying every moment of this special treat.

While they know who their real parents are, Mbuti children become accustomed from an early age to expecting parental care and attention—including both discipline and love—from every adult in an Mbuti hunting camp. Living as they do in a relatively hostile environment, life for the Mbuti is not always as utopian as it may seem, and the average life span could be as low as thirty years. (Some say forty years.) The band survives against seemingly overwhelming odds through constant, communal effort, and the well-being of each child is in the best interests of the band as a whole.

It is a measure of the closeness of the people in an Mbuti camp that each child calls every man father and every woman mother (or grandfather or grandmother if they are old). Mbuti children cannot conceive of an existence without the extended family. Grandparents are expected to live with their children and grandchildren. Those in the younger generation in turn expect to enjoy the company of their grandparents for as long as the old people live. I have never seen a happier little girl than Deta as she sat being painted by the one she called grandmother.

As for Bakbara, her own children and grandchildren were lost to her forever, for they would seldom if ever leave the village to visit her in the forest. I had often seen her sitting sad and lonely by herself, gazing vacantly at nothing in particular, perhaps dreaming of what might have been.

That same day, Mazero decided to cut the hair of her husband, Mokono. It appeared that somebody had found a good sharpening stone, for the camp knives seemed to be particularly sharp at once. Even old Ndima sat outside his hut having his wispy beard cut by his wife, Sibaku.

Near my hut, Alita was painting Maguti's body in the fashion the Efe call *ebembe*. Starting with her friend's wrists, Alita ran a line of black dots along her arms and down her chest to the center of both breasts, playfully dabbing a spot of paint on each nipple when she came to the end of the line. Then, still using her fingers as a brush, she began to paint circles on Maguti's buttocks.

I decided that since the camp was apparently in a mood for personal hygiene and cosmetic endeavors, I might as well join in the activity and attempt to trim my beard. Among the items that I did not share with the camp was a pair of scissors which

I kept with the medicines. Another irreplaceable belonging I did not share was a small mirror. Both items were the only ones in camp, and if once shared I would never get them back.

After I had tried with little success to prop the mirror on my knees, Alita noticed my predicament and came over to hold the mirror for me. Both she and Maguti found it all quite amusing, and their laughter soon brought Sukali over, who immediately suggested that if Alita would cut my hair the way a good wife should, I would not have such a problem. With that he took the mirror from Alita and wandered off, admiring the reflection of his face.

Alita had never held a pair of scissors in her hand before, but after a brief demonstration from me, she learned quickly and began to trim my beard to the length I suggested. A few people came over and watched curiously for a while, but soon the novelty wore off and Alita was able to concentrate on her task. I have had my hair cut in many strange places on several continents but never with a barber so exotic as Alita. Bare-breasted and recently painted all over, she was wielding a pair of scissors for the first time in her life. She was so tiny that she had to reach upward to work, although I was sitting down. When she had finished, I looked around for Sukali, but he and the mirror were nowhere to be seen.

But Alita had not yet finished. Dragging over a log to stand on, she placed the back of my head against her bosom and fondly began to groom me like a mother with her child, or a girl with her boyfriend. It was somewhat embarrassing, for to Alita, to groom meant to meticulously and patiently search my head for lice. However, after a while I began to enjoy the sensation of her probing fingers and would probably have fallen asleep if my chair had been more comfortable. If a barber like Alita was a first for me, then having my head publicly examined for lice was certainly another. Idly, I wondered if her body paint was dry.

From where I sat I watched two little girls of about seven playing dolls with a real baby. They took turns alternately holding it in a nursing position against their chests and carrying it in a sling over their shoulder. When the baby became restless, they lay on their backs and bounced it up and down on their stomachs until it squealed with pleasure. It was the only doll the children would ever have, and their play was also a learning experience for when they would have children of their own. But mother was always watching and listening for the plaintive cry of her hungry infant and from time to time would intrude long enough to nurse it in the way that the children could not.

The games Mbuti children play are frequently an imitation of adult behavior. Little boys only three years old are given tiny bows and arrows by proud fathers and quite seriously stalk and kill butterflies and toads. In time, they graduate to birds and small mammals and reptiles. By the time they reach their early teens, they are quite capable of killing enough meat for their personal needs and can often be seen cooking their catch over their own fires. Sometimes a prepubescent boy and girl will build their own little hut at the edge of the camp and play father and mother. They'll borrow a pot and go through a ritual of preparing and cooking things they brought back from the forest. On one occasion, I saw such a young couple pretending to copulate in a way so realistic that they could only have learned by observing adults doing the real thing.

On going through my medicines that morning, I had found four balloons that I had packed and forgotten. But when I blew three of them up and released them, the children never got a chance to play with these exotic objects. Instead, every hunter in the camp hurried over and began a hilarious game of bouncing the balloons in the air and to each other. Even Asumali and Ndeke joined in the fun, competing with Arumbu, the elephant hunter, who leaped higher than anybody else. As the children watched and wondered, the grown men boisterously chased the balloons all over camp until they all eventually burst. After a few moments curiously examining the deflated fragments, each hunter returned to what he had been doing previously and the camp was quiet again.

After I blew up the fourth balloon, which was bright red, I walked over and placed it directly in the hands of one of the little girls who was playing with the baby. Like the hunters, she had never seen anything like it in her entire life. Within moments every child in camp was wildly chasing it among the huts until it too exploded with a loud pop. Later I saw its tattered remains hanging as an ornament from a girl's belt instead of the customary decorative green leaves.

Not long afterward Arumbu came seeking medicine for his ailing father, who apparently had become too weak to come and see me himself. Ndima was obviously quite old, and I regretted that I did not know the precise nature of his illness. I could treat a tropical ulcer, superficial wounds, malaria, and even deliver a baby, but I was not equipped with the knowledge or materials to do much more. However, as Ndima usually only complained of general aches, I brought along some aspirin tablets when I went to see him in his hut.

Inside I found the old man lying on a bed made of only three wooden poles laid on the ground. In typical Mbuti fashion, his arm was his pillow. I was dismayed that his appearance was worse than before. His ribs showed clearly through his skin and his fine, intelligent eyes had retreated deeper into his skull. At my request Ndima's wife, Sibaku, scooped some water into a mongongo leaf, and with this he gratefully swallowed the aspirin I placed in his unwashed hand.

I looked around Ndima's hut and was reminded of how little an Mbuti owns after a lifetime of hard work in the forest. The two cooking pots outside belonged to Sibaku, as did the wooden mortar and the knife stuck in her belt. He did not even have on his tattered bark cloth but lay wrinkled and naked on his side, looking up at me with his gentle eyes. Against the smoke-blackened wall of the hut stood the old nomad's well-worn bow, a proud reminder of his days as a hunter. Beside it the quiver lay empty. Except for his traditional temporary one-roomed family hut of sticks and leaves, the bow he had once made with his own hands was the only material thing he owned in the world.

But Ndima was not aware that he had so little. Indeed, he probably thought of himself as having everything an old man could wish to have, for he had his children and grandchildren living around him.

I sat on a mat of mongongo leaves beside him. "How are you, Father?" I asked.

Ndima gestured feebly toward his emaciated body. "I am tired," he said simply.

I reached for his bow and examined it. "When are you going to take me hunting?" I inquired after a moment.

Ndima smiled. "Tomorrow," he said. "Tomorrow we will go into the forest together and kill a monkey."

Outside, I found the women busy at their huts, preparing the evening meal. Bakbara, with the shaven head, had undertaken to make the palm-oil sauce from the palm nuts collected by all the women in the forest, the same women whose younger children she looked after during the day. She no longer accompanied the more active women on their arduous gathering trips, and this was one way for her to contribute to the group effort, for the pot of bright yellow liquid she had extracted from the nuts by pounding in a mortar would be shared by all. She had willing helpers among the children, to whom mouthfuls of the fibrous pulp left over after the pounding was enjoyed endlessly like chewing gum.

I watched Lehilehi remove the fur from the monkey her husband had shot by placing it directly on the fire until most of the hair was burned off. Then, after removing its intestines, she put the monkey into a large pot with some water and put it on the fire to boil. It did not improve my appetite to see the fingers of one little hand seemingly grip the rim of the pot and a pair of near-human eyes peering up at me through the water.

Another common method of cooking meat in Mbuti camps is to put it directly on the hot embers to roast. Yet another way—and the one I personally prefer—is to impale a piece of meat on a stick, which is then driven into the ground at an angle over the flames to roast clear of the ashes.

Nothing is wasted among the Mbuti. I watched Lehilehi wrap the intestines of the monkey in leaves and put them directly on the edge of the fire to roast, just as I have seen done with the intestines and brains of antelope. Even the skin is eaten and eventually the bones are cracked open for their marrow. I was glad to see that Lehilehi first squeezed out the contents of the intestines before wrapping them in the leaves.

That evening I dined well on snake and monkey, both of which were enhanced with caterpillars roasted in the leaf, two kinds of mushrooms, and one kind of grub boiled in palm oil. Eating with one's fingers directly from the pot and from mongongo leaves placed on the ground somehow added to the flavor, which for me at least was exotic.

The people I shared the meal with included Ndeke and his married daughter, who was visiting from another camp with her year-old infant son. The little boy had been nursing on her breast when he became restless and began to reach up toward his mother's mouth as she ate. At first she appeared to be ignoring the child as she carefully chewed what was in her mouth. Then she leaned down to his upturned, expectant face and seemed to give her son a long, passionate kiss full on the mouth. She did this twice before I realized that she was passing premasticated food from her own mouth into his. Only after she had done this several times did the child seem to be satisfied and again grabbed one of her breasts in his grubby hands to suckle contentedly once more. I must have seen such an occurrence many times at a greater distance and did not realize its significance.

While adult Mbuti do not usually kiss each other—on the lips or elsewhere—mothers often kiss their young children, and I wondered which came first—kissing out of playfulness, love, and affection (which they do often) or making mouth contact out of a desire to supplement breast milk with solid food.

However, even with the supplement of premasticated food, which parallels factory-made baby foods in modern society, Mbuti women continue to nurse their children for about two years. Indeed, I have sometimes seen an older child steal a little milk from one breast of an indulgent mother while she was nursing her latest infant on the other. It is not surprising to find that love of parents is a strong trait among the Mbuti and that it lasts as long as the parents are alive. In *Among Congo Pigmies* (1929), Schebesta wrote, " . . . It is the custom for a young man returning home after a long stay away, to seek his mother at once and to fondle her bosom as he was wont to do as a baby. This act is regarded as a special token of affection and tenderness."

In *Wayward Servants* (1965) Turnbull says that "To swear at someone by accusing them of having sex with their parent is mild; it is more serious to accuse them of having sex with their sibling of one stomach. (Same mother). Worst of all is to accuse someone of having sex with her or his spouse." He adds that "The degree of freedom between sons and mothers may be seen in the fact that a mother gives strength to her children, if they are ill, by sleeping in the same bed with them. This is sometimes done between a mother and her adult son, so long as he is unmarried, without occasioning any comment."

Filial love is a response also to the uninhibited fondness with which Mbuti fathers treat their children. There is no shame or embarrassment on the part of a man in fondling a child, male or female, and the children expect and desire it. To both child and man, such an expression of love is entirely natural, and the fact that they are virtually naked is of no consequence whatsoever, for to the Mbuti, this too is natural.

That was the evening when Mateso went into labor, an expected event, which was in itself not a cause for alarm. Unfortunately it was also the evening that a wide column of deadly safari ants invaded the camp. These vicious on the march insects have only one purpose: to kill, tear apart, and carry off the pieces of every living, edible creature in their path. This can include anything from a grounded butterfly to a sleeping human to an immobilized elephant. Safari ants do not know the meaning of fear or size and are mindlessly suicidal in their food-gathering rampages. Although they are frequently encountered during the day, they dislike direct sunlight and usually attack at night, the time when humans and many other creatures are most vulnerable to this silent, creeping death.

But first there was Mateso. Everybody had retired for the

night to their respective huts when she apparently began to experience her first real labor pains. Nothing is private in an Mbuti camp, and her groans, gasps, and whimpers were heard and understood by all. But after the first hour of such sounds, there were additional cries of distress. The safari ants had attacked.

"Ants! Ants!" The warning cries of Lehilehi, who was attending the birth, awakened the entire camp and within moments everybody was dashing about in the darkness, waving smoldering sticks as makeshift torches, trying to locate the main column of ants advancing out of the forest with its millions of aggressive soldiers. Using leaves, pieces of bark, and anything they could find, men, women, and children were quickly scooping up ashes and hot embers from the fires and throwing them on the ground to form a barrier between the camp and the attacking column.

I was glad that I had saved my flashlight for emergencies, and with it I helped Arumbu see that his hut and the one next to it were being totally overrun by ants. Mateso was in the throes of labor, yet was forced to abandon everything and retreat naked and defenseless to Lehilehi's hut, which stood next to mine. As she walked, she frantically slapped her thighs and tore ants from her body. I wondered if the birth fluids had been some kind of signal that had drawn the ants to the attack.

Ignoring the yelling and frantic activity directed at repelling the ants, I heeded Lehilehi's call to bring the light and joined her in the otherwise total darkness of her hut. There I held the light as Lehilehi plucked ants from all over Mateso's body while at the same time helping her into a position to give birth. Some of the ants' pincers were buried so deeply in Mateso's skin that their heads remained embedded after their bodies were torn away.

There is little inclination on the part of the Mbuti to cling to traditional ways in the event of a medical emergency. Unlike the taboo-ridden villagers, the Mbuti respond to someone in distress with a quick acceptance of whatever practical help is available. Firelight is better than darkness, and in this case the

Muzungu with his flashlight was better than firelight. Like other women I had happened to attend in childbirth, Mateso cared little about who was present, and her one compelling thought was to expel the baby. She sat on a small piece of wood just four fingers high with her feet on the ground and her knees drawn up against her swollen belly. With each contraction, Lehilehi watched carefully for the baby's head, her hand ready to guide it onto the mat of leaves that lay directly on the ground beneath Mateso's distended vulva.

Outside, the war continued against the ants, with familiar voices yelling to bring more ashes, to build bigger fires, to keep the small children safe. In the general commotion it was difficult to tell if the ants were winning or not, and from time to time I nervously checked the floor of the hut to see if they had reached it.

In the birth hut, I conserved the flashlight's battery by switching it off between contractions, and hoped that the baby would come before the batteries ran out. But there was to be another problem before the night was over. For some time thunder and lightning had been coming closer, and I was dreading the possibility of a deluge adding to the nightmare of the killer safari ants.

The rain began moments after a searing lightning flash and deafening thunderclap exploded overhead. It was not just rain, but a torrential downpour accompanied by repeated lightning and thunder that obliterated all visibility and sounds outside. Thankfully it was heavy enough to discourage the ants from invading farther than the hut from which Mateso had been evicted.

I made room as Lehilehi's youngest daughter, Nasi, and Mateso's daughter, Deta, both dashed in from the rain. They were quickly followed by Mokono's wife, Mazero. Minutes later we were all witnesses to the birth of Mateso's newest child.

The head began to appear and Mateso pushed hard one more time. When the head popped out, Lehilehi caught it in her hands and gently eased the baby onto the ground as it slid smoothly from the mother's body. It was a little boy and he almost immediately took his first breath and began to cry lustily without any encouragement from Lehilehi. He had arrived in the Mbuti world, and the first thing he lay on was the floor of the forest. By the time the placenta was delivered and he was suckling from his mother's breast, it was already dawn and the beginning of another day in the Ituri.

A few days later I visited Ndima and found him weaker than ever. He had been helped outside his hut by his wife, Sibaku, and lay on a mat of woven leaves at the fire. I sat on a log beside him.

"How are you, Father?" I inquired gently.

Ndima held out his hand for his daily aspirin. "I am sick. I need more medicine."

I held up the almost empty aspirin bottle to this old man who was clearly dying. "Look, Father, the medicine is nearly finished. I can only give you one each day. And besides, you're going to get better soon."

Ndima shook his head sadly. "I have been sick before and got better. This time I will not get better. Now I am an old man and will never see another camp." He waved toward his simple shelter, which had become brown and withered. "I have lived in many huts since I was born in the forest. But this is the last camp I will ever see, and this is the hut where I will die."

I glanced at Sibaku, who was sitting with us, but she did not speak and her face was expressionless as she stooped down to rearrange the fire.

Along with everybody else in the camp, I looked up when the drone of an airplane sounded in the distance. It was very seldom that an aircraft of any kind was heard over the remote Ituri and even more seldom that it could actually be seen from the floor of the forest through a gap in the trees unless it happened to pass directly overhead.

That day the sound of the plane came closer and closer until it was apparent that it would pass right over the camp. When it finally appeared, it was flying high, a silvery speck floating alone in the brilliant tropical sky. From such a height the forest was an endless horizon-to-horizon wilderness of sweltering, haze-covered green with the puffy texture and density of a cauliflower. Only an occasional river parted the giant trees. Beneath their canopy, meandering streams flowed quietly and were not seen.

To the pilot above us, Camp Tupi was invisible except for a trace of smoke filtering through the treetops. He never saw our faces staring curiously toward the sky, and we never saw his. Within hours he would reach his destination in another world far beyond the Ituri, a destination that could take a man on foot months to reach.

Ndima lay on the floor of the forest, his eyes following the plane through the trees. To him it was an *ndege*—literally, a bird, simply because there was no word in his language for airplane.

"Do you know what that is?" I asked him, referring to the plane.

"It's an ndege," he said, as if surprised that I should ask such a question.

"But what kind of ndege?" I asked.

Ndima turned his head to look toward the receding sound of the plane's engines and hesitated for only a moment while he sought the right words. "It's a *kamio* [truck] with wings so that it can fly."

"Who is inside it?"

Ndima shrugged. "*Wazunga* [Europeans]."

"Have you ever seen an ndege on the ground?"

The old man shook his head. "No. I have seen them only in the sky."

"How do you know there are people inside it?"

"Because," Ndima said, "the men who drive the kamios on the road told me so."

Just then Ndima's son Arumbu and his daughter-in-law Mateso, carrying their newborn son, wandered over from their hut to join us. This meant that I was in the company of three generations of an extended Mbuti family.

Ndima looked up toward the baby in Mateso's arms. "What will you call my grandson?" he asked querulously.

Arumbu looked uncomfortable. "It is not yet time to give him a name," he said, referring to the traditional delay in naming Mbuti infants until they have survived the first critical period—usually many weeks—after their birth.

To my surprise Ndima turned to me. "When Arumbu was born," he said with quiet disdain, "I gave him a name the same day . . . the name of Arumbu, his grandfather!"

I caught Arumbu's eye and thought I saw him smile. This was a very personal matter between father and son, but in typical Mbuti fashion it was being aired for all to hear. Ndima looked up at me again. "Perhaps you can give the child a name." He shrugged. "You saw the child being born, you give it a name."

I glanced from Mateso to her husband, Arumbu, the renowned elephant hunter whose word was the most respected in the band. Both parents returned my glance expectantly, and I was startled to realize that they both wanted me to do as Ndima requested. It was a rare honor, and several names, some exotic, others personal, occurred to me almost immediately: Alexander, Maxwell, Patrick, Caesar, Homer, Stanley.

These were all fine names, but I rejected them after only a moment's consideration. "The name I give the child," I said at last, "is Ndima Kidogo—Little Ndima."

Arumbu slapped his knee. "Good, very good," he exclaimed gleefully, turning to Mateso, who readily smiled her approval. I smiled in return and was glad that I had made a choice apparently popular with everybody concerned.

This was not an occasion that happened every day in Camp Tupi, and I looked around to find that a small crowd had silently and respectfully gathered to witness this event in the life of the band's oldest member. But Ndima did not seem to notice anybody but his grandson as he reached out a frail arm for assistance. We helped him to sit up and watched as Mateso tenderly put the infant in his arms.

Nobody spoke as Ndima sat gently rocking his grandson to and fro. "Ndima Kidogo," the old man murmured while tenderly pressing the tiny infant against his worn out, wrinkled body. "I will make your first bow, and we will hunt together in the forest."

I wondered if Ndima knew that the hunting around Camp Tupi had become poor and that the only reason why the band did not move to a new location was because of his inability to walk.

Early that evening we heard an owl calling close to the camp, and the more fearless among the hunters threw burning logs in the direction and shouted at it to go away. But the next night it returned after everybody had retired for the night, and this time the people apprehensively stayed in their huts and were silent. They knew that the owl was an incarnation of the darker side of Tore, who was not only lord of the forest, but also lord of the dead. The owl's cry was feared because it meant that somebody would soon die.

I lay in my hut, listening to the lonely call of the hunter owl and remembering that the soul of the one who died would be taken by Tore to stay with him forever as a Lodi in the invisible spirit world, which coexisted in the forest with the physical world of the Mbuti. In the darkness of the hut, it was not difficult to believe what the Mbuti believed. The familiar elements of my own culture were thousands of miles away in another world and could almost have been a figment of my imagination.

Three days after the owl first called, Ndima was dead. Sibaku's anguished wailing at dawn, when she was unable to wake him, quickly aroused the entire camp. Most of those who rushed from their huts were as naked as Sibaku, who was standing outside her hut, beating her fists against her bony chest, sobbing pitifully.

Soon most of the women and children in camp were grouped around her, wailing just as loudly. Arumbu pushed past the women into the death hut. When he emerged minutes later, this strong and usually silent man was crying like a child. The kind and gentle father he had known all his life was dead and the hoarse screams of the elephant hunter were terrible to hear. Running naked to his hut, he tore it apart stick by stick until there was nothing left. Then, turning to some logs that were lying nearby, he flung them one by one and with great force into the forest while still screaming his terrible screams. Only then did he become quiet and seek out his mother and hold her in his strong arms.

But Sibaku was inconsolable. The person who had been her husband and closest companion for most of her life was gone forever. He was the one who had fathered her children and who had matched her baskets of wild foods with monkey and antelope meat for almost as long as she could remember. When Ndima died, part of her died too, and nothing anybody could do could change that. All the talk of megbe immortality and totem reincarnations meant little to a woman who knew she would sleep alone the rest of her life.

I joined Ndeke where he was building up a fire outside his hut. He had put on his belt and bark cloth and seemed relatively composed. Yet when he sat down on a log beside me, there were tears trickling down his lined face. His was a silent grief, and I was well aware that he had chosen to live with this particular Efe band because it included both Ndima, his lifelong favorite cousin, and Ndima's son Arumbu, the best hunter in the area.

In Camp Tupi every man and his children were related to Ndima, and even the wives who had come from other bands had known the old man all their lives. Such an Mbuti band was like a large extended family, and there was no man, woman, or child who did not feel a deep personal loss.

Later that same morning, Mangoma and some of the young hunters dug a shallow grave inside Ndima's hut, using only knives as tools. When the tedious work was completed, they lay the body on its side in the grave with a small log tenderly placed under the head as a pillow. Then they reverently covered it with leaves before beginning to push the loose earth back into place with their bare hands.

Twice Sibaku tried to throw herself into the grave with her dead husband, and each time she was restrained and dragged back. She wailed incessantly, usually accompanied by at least one other sympathetically wailing woman friend or relative.

Meanwhile, Arumbu sat at the central fire, which had been ritually rekindled despite the community tragedy. He stared into its flames and talked to no one. Only when the final handful of earth was put on the body and the grave diggers had emerged did he pick up two flaming logs from the fire and slowly walk toward the hut where his dead father lay.

There were no prayers or incantations over the grave, and only the crying and keening of the women told the forest that one of its children had died. For Ndima, there would be no eulogy listing his fine qualities and life's achievements, no one to say that he was too gentle to have been a great hunter like his son or that he had been kind, generous, and wise and was loved by his family and his friends. It was not necessary to say these things or even to invent them, because they were true and already well-known by all.

Arumbu crouched down beside the wall of the hut and placed the burning logs against its dried and withered leaves. Within moments flames flared up, and before long the entire hut became a blazing funeral pyre.

Sibaku tried to throw herself into the flames, but Arumbu seemed to expect this and stood between his mother and the burning hut. When she tried again, he held her tightly in his arms, where she did not resist any further but instead pressed her face into his hairy chest and sobbed uncontrollably.

The initial mourning for Ndima would end almost as soon as the burial and burning of the hut was completed, not because Ndima was unloved, but because a nomadic band of Mbuti in the forest couldn't afford to mourn any longer. None of the women or girls had gone gathering in the forest that day, nor had any of the men or boys hunted. Except for a few scraps, there was no food in the entire camp, and the only way to obtain more was to go out into the forest and work for it. Yet because of the burial—and because game was becoming scarce in the area—it was decided by general agreement that we would abandon Camp Tupi for good that same day. Ndima had ceased to be a community burden, and the living had to continue their effort to stay alive.

Soon after the flames of the hut had died away, everybody was tying his or her few possessions into bundles and preparing to move to a new campsite somewhere in the forest. Somebody told me where we were going, but the name of our destination was meaningless to me. I put my own things in a pile outside my hut and was pleased and grateful when Sukali sauntered over to where I was working and, without a word, selected one of my two backpacks, which he clearly intended to carry for me. Then, just like an anthropologist or archaeologist, he curiously went through every scrap of rubbish that had accumulated in my hut since I first arrived in Camp Tupi.

Nothing was spared his intense scrutiny. Every scrap of paper was opened up and examined on both sides. Discarded medicinal foil containers and bottles were scrutinized minutely. The colorful wrappers of some of my long-gone emergency rations were of special interest to him. He could not read a word on these torn wrappers but could tell by sniffing them that they had once contained exotic substances that were good to eat. I had earlier shared a small part of these items with him until they ran out, but his reproachful glances toward me as he examined my little mound of trash telegraphed his suspicions that I had been enjoying banqueting orgies without him. The truth of the matter was that I had actually lost much of my normal body weight and was depending on my usually good health to allow me to survive intact until I eventually walked out of the forest.

From my trash pile Sukali selected an empty aspirin bottle and a plastic bag, both of which he kept for himself, and distributed the few colorful wrappers he found to some children who had curiously gathered to observe his archaeological "dig." Even in the presence of death, the exuberant Mbuti sense of humor and skill in mimicry could not be denied. One little boy made a notebook out of a folded piece of paper, and with a slender stick for a pencil he adopted an exaggerated scholarly manner and pretended to take anthropological notes while interviewing his fellow playmates.

As nomads, this little Mbuti band had few possessions, and

the heaviest loads on a migratory move through the forest were the children who were too young to walk. Mothers carried unweaned infants in shoulder slings of bark cloth or animal skin, which allowed the child to rest on the hip or be swung around to the front to be breast-fed when necessary. Each woman also carried the inevitable basket suspended by a bark strap from just above the forehead. These baskets contained all their family's worldly goods—pots, an occasional wooden mortar, sometimes a precious piece of cloth to cover their nakedness when visiting a roadside village. Their baskets would also be used to collect any wild foods found along the way while the hunters ranged far ahead in the hope of killing an animal for the evening meal. One other thing to be carried was the smoldering logs without which there would be no fire at the new camp.

Any child between the approximate ages of two and four was carried in a sling by an older sibling or cousin, traditionally a girl. There would be no arguments about who would or would not carry. If a girl was unavailable to carry a younger child, a boy or even a hunter would be readily willing to do so. Among the Mbuti there is no sexual division of labor so important that it cannot be treated with indifference when the welfare of the band or one of its members is at stake.

What was necessary now was to march for several miles through the muddy wilderness of the rain forest, to somehow make the forest give up enough food to feed a hungry band, and finally, to defy a possible rainstorm while building shelters out of sticks and leaves. All this had to be done before dark, and on the same day we had buried Ndima. I hoped that rain wouldn't extinguish the smoldering logs being carried, for I shared an inability with the Mbuti to make fire without matches.

# 8

## Elephant Hunt

One day soon after we had settled in the new camp, the hunters returned from the forest to announce that they had found fresh elephant tracks. That evening around the fire the matter was discussed and argued back and forth.

"The forest," Ndeke gravely told the others, "is sad since the death of Ndima. To kill an elephant would make it happy again. We would meet everybody who came to share the meat and there would be much singing and dancing."

Mokono spoke up next. "I will kill the elephant!" he exclaimed, jumping up to demonstrate how he would perform this mighty feat. Picking up a stick, he crept forward and thrust it violently into an imaginary animal while everybody laughed appreciatively.

"You don't even own a spear," Asumali told him sarcastically, "and besides, you've never killed an elephant before."

Ndeke spoke again. "There is one person who has a spear, and he has killed an elephant before now." There was a general murmur of agreement and everybody turned expectantly to the one among them to whom Ndeke referred.

Arumbu finally looked up and glanced from face to face before replying. "Today I saw the tracks of a big elephant," he said quietly. "Tomorrow I will follow the tracks and kill that elephant with my spear."

Mapoli jumped up and began to beat the drum without bothering to tighten its skin over the flames of the fire. The Mbuti's zest for living is never far below the surface, and now it exploded in a frenzy of celebration as everybody joined in the singing and dancing. Even before elephant hunting was declared illegal in the Ituri, the actual killing of one of these beasts by a spear-wielding Mbuti was a relatively rare event. Not every band included a hunter willing or skillful enough to pit himself against the largest animal in the forest, and most Mbuti knew of a friend or relative who had died horribly when attempting to do so. Yet in their precarious, hardworking existence, the Mbuti tend to think positively. When Arumbu said he would kill an elephant, then he and the others believed that he would.

That evening there were stirring hunting songs, and there were also songs that prayed to the forest for a successful hunt. There were special dances in which those participating played the parts of the elephant and the hunters. In such dances the hunters always won against their formidable adversary.

The next morning I sat with the men when they met around the central fire to share a ceremonial drink made from the kola nut, a fruit containing theobromine and which once provided the caffeine stimulant used in Coca-Cola and other soft drinks. Mixed with certain green berries from the forest, the properties of which I do not know, we drank this concoction, which had at least the effect of very strong coffee. As the camp did not possess cups or other drinking vessels, each man used a cupped leaf to scoop his share from the common pot in which the mixture had been boiled. And so a bond of friendship was strengthened between a group of hunters, just as it might have been thousands of years ago in the same primeval forest. There would be a personal triumph—or tragedy—for the man who thrust the spear into the elephant. But everyone knew that if the hunt went well, the meat would be shared by all.

In the event of a successful hunt, the festivities that followed would exceed any other joyous occasion in the forest. For days and even weeks afterward there would be no serious hunting as everybody joined in a continuous orgy of eating. Nomadic bands that perhaps had not met for a year would join together. Unrelated young men and women of different clans would have the opportunity for uninhibited romantic encounters, and perhaps some would find permanent marriage partners. There would be singing and dancing as the people thanked the forest for its benevolence and for sparing the life of the hunter—if it was spared.

I gave Arumbu a steel file I had so far managed to keep in reserve. He had never used such a tool before, but in a moment he was carefully sharpening the dull, rusted blade of his spear, and I could see that he was very pleased with this unexpected present. When he had finished, the spear had been transformed into a gleaming weapon so sharp that one of the hunters cut his finger in testing it.

Preparations for the hunt included the darkening of the hunters' faces with a black paste. According to the hunters, when the elephant sees them thus disguised among the shadows it will think they are chimpanzees and so ignore them. The preparations also included wrapping some food in leaves and hanging these bundles from the hunters' waists, for the elephant hunt could mean spending one or more nights in the forest away from the camp.

When Arumbu finally departed, he was accompanied only by the two strongest of the hunters, Sukali and his drummer brother, Mapoli, who carried a smoldering log so that they would have fire. I had been with and filmed Mbuti hunters on a successful elephant hunt nearly ten years earlier in another part of the Ituri (for my film *Pygmies of the Rain Forest*). Even then, despite my greater youth and relatively extensive experience in the hunting of these pachyderms in Zambia, I soon realized that no ordinary man could keep pace with an Mbuti once he decided to catch up with and kill an elephant in the difficult conditions of a rain forest. Unlike smaller animals, the heavy elephant always leaves clear tracks on the ever damp and often muddy floor of the forest, and what makes the Mbuti a particularly deadly hunter of these beasts is not just his keen tracking eye and extraordinary stealth, but also his physical ability to run mile after mile in pursuit of a prey that leaves such obvious tracks.

On this occasion I did not attempt to accompany the elephant hunters, but instead remained in camp and watched some of the women leave with their baskets on a foraging trip into the forest while the remaining hunters went off one by one with their bows after monkeys and small game. Among those who did not go into the forest that day were the old ladies of the band, Sibaku and Bakbara. Each was optimistically making a rattan basket to help carry the meat of the elephant.

The basket may well have been the most important invention in the Mbuti's evolution since the advent of speech. Without it, the gathering efforts of a band were limited to what they could carry in their hands, unless they ate what they found on the spot like wild animals. With the basket it became possible to more efficiently utilize the vast area that surrounded them and bring back food to a central point—the organized camp that made the development of their culture possible.

While an antelope could be slung across the shoulders and easily carried, meat was still probably only an occasional luxury, especially before the appearance of the bow, the metal-bladed spear, and—among the Sua—the hunting net. It is likely that the early Mbuti obtained much of their protein from crustaceans easily gathered by hand from the streams and from seeds, snakes, flying termites, and the larvae of various insects, which are still considered delicacies today.

Without the basket, such items as caterpillars, berries, fruits, nuts, roots, leafy vegetables, mushrooms, crabs, and crayfish would be difficult to transport each day to wherever the nomadic band had chosen to make camp. With the basket, an individual could carry more than was needed for personal use and so share with others. Along with the sharing of the meat of any animals killed, this was the beginning of the general and economic reciprocity that would become such a fundamental part of the human way of life.

The Mbuti say that the chimpanzees are not human because

they do not use fire. It could also be said that they are not human because they have never learned to use a receptacle or basket for carrying and storing food and must eat it where and when it is found.

I joined Ndeke where he sat, smoking a pipe at the fire. "Have you ever hunted elephants?" I asked him.

"Yes," he said. "When I was young I went hunting with my brother and he was killed by the elephant I wounded."

"Killed completely?"

"Yes," Ndeke said quietly. "Killed completely."

"Did the elephant die?"

Ndeke shook his head. "I don't know. It ran away and I did not follow."

"Do you think Arumbu will kill an elephant today?"

"Arumbu has killed elephants before. He is a very good hunter and I think he will kill one today or tomorrow."

We sat for a while before Ndeke spoke again. "Do people hunt elephants in your country?" he asked.

"A very long time ago the people in my country used to hunt a kind of elephant that was bigger than the elephant here in the forest. It was called a mammoth."

"Mam–moth?" Ndeke repeated curiously. "It was bigger than an elephant?"

"It *was* an elephant, but a different kind, just as the Lese and the Bambuti are both people, but the Lese are bigger."

Ndeke pondered this for a moment. "Have you ever killed such a big elephant?" he asked thoughtfully.

"No," I said. "But I have killed elephants in Africa."

"Afri–kah?"

"It's a place outside the forest," I told him.

"Tell me about places outside the forest," Ndeke, the story-teller, asked, inviting me to exchange roles.

"At the top of the world," I said, "there are hunters called Eskimos who live in a place where there are no trees, and who kill animals that live in a great water."

"No trees?" Ndeke exclaimed incredulously.

"No trees," I emphasized, remembering my stay with the polar, or Thule, Eskimos in northern Greenland, the most northerly dwelling people in the world. "And their women can't gather any food because there is none for them to gather."

"No food?"

"There is no food that grows on the land because the ground is bare like Bakbara's head," I explained as best I could, wondering if I should try to describe snow, ice, and cold that can kill.

"What do the people eat?"

"The hunters kill the animals and fish that live in the water," I said.

"What kind of animals?"

"Whales and seals and walruses," I told him.

"Are there any animals like them in the forest?"

"No," I said. "They are not the same."

"Are there any elephants?"

"There are no elephants because there are no trees."

"If there are no trees," Ndeke asked curiously, "how do they make fire?"

"They don't have fire, only a small light they make from the fat of the animals they kill."

"No fire?" Ndeke exclaimed. "No trees, no food for the women to gather. That is a very bad place!"

"Also," I said, "sometimes the sun stays up in the sky for many moons without going away, and the people must sleep when it is light. And sometimes," I added, "the sun leaves the sky for many moons and the people must stay in darkness every day."

Ndeke stared at me. He probably wondered if this was just some harmless Muzungu folklore or if he was really supposed to believe it. When at last he spoke, it was to ask me a logical question that could indicate if I spoke the truth or not.

"Have you been there . . . to this place with no trees?"

"Yes," I told him gravely. "I have been there. That is how I know."

"What else did you see in the place without trees?" the old

man asked, apparently deciding that he might as well hear it all.

"Well," I said, "it is so cold that the cold can kill people."

"Cold can kill people?"

"Yes," I told him, "it is so cold that there is no water because the cold makes it into something hard which is called ice. You can eat it but you cannot drink it."

This time Ndeke simply did not believe me. "No trees!" he said reprovingly. "No fire! No water! Cold that can kill! The sun stays in the sky all night!"

"There is one other strange thing about the place of no trees," I could not resist adding. "It never rains there."

At this, Ndeke smiled knowingly, as one accomplished, imaginative storyteller to another. "That is certainly a terrible place," he said. "Tell me about other strange places you have visited."

I knew that Ndeke was enjoying our conversation and that whatever stories I told would be repeated and embellished around the camp fires long after I had left the forest, just as I would repeat his. I had grown to love this old man who had never quite killed an elephant and who possessed a vast store of knowledge about his environment I could only begin to understand in my brief visit from my world to his. But now he waited expectantly for my reply.

"In a place far from here beyond the mountains," I said, pointing east toward Uganda and Kenya, "there are people who call themselves the Pokot, just as your people call themselves the Bambuti. There is so little water in their country that they sometimes pray to their god to send rain. They do this by killing a goat with a spear and offering it to their god so that the rain will come."

"Have you seen them do this?" Ndeke asked shrewdly.

"Yes, I have been there and I have seen it."

"What other kinds of people have you seen?"

"I have been with the Hadza people in Tanzania. They have bows and arrows much bigger than those of the Bambuti, and they can kill animals at a great distance."

"Do they use poison on their arrows?"

"No," I told him. "I did not see them using poison. The arrows are so big that they can kill without it."

Ndeke waited expectantly for more.

"In another country where I have been," I continued, "there are people who are called bedouins. They are Arabs who live in a place where there is only sand and no trees."

"Do they hunt animals?"

"Very little," I said. "It is hot in the place where the bedouins live, and there is little water and no rain and nothing for animals to eat."

"Do these people look like Bambuti?"

"No, the bedouins do not look like the Bambuti but," I said, pointing south, "very far in that direction live the bushmen, who look like the Bambuti and who hunt the animals just as the Bambuti do. They use poison on their arrows, and their women gather food in baskets just like the women of the Bambuti."

"Are there trees in that place?"

"Yes, there are a few trees, but they are very small."

"So they have fire?" Ndeke asked hopefully.

"Yes, they have fire, and they sing and dance, and they are great hunters, just like the Bambuti."

Ndeke smiled, happy at last to find that there was a people somewhere in the outside world who could be his cousins. Then a thought occurred to him. "These people," he asked carefully, "are they tall like the Lese?"

"No," I told him. "They are a small people, about the same size as the Bambuti."

Ndeke smiled even more broadly. For the next half-hour he questioned me closely about how the bushmen lived, their hunting techniques, and what animals they hunted.

By nightfall Arumbu and the two hunters with him had not returned from the elephant hunt. The people waited quietly around the fires, listening for any sign from the darkened forest. But all they could hear was the dismal howl of a hyrax and the

Mbuti playing antique trumpet carved from ivory elephant tusk.

Playing musical instrument of a design of great antiquity.

Mbuti spectators watching a dance.

Molimo trumpet.

Celebrating the kill.

Hunters with the slain elephant.

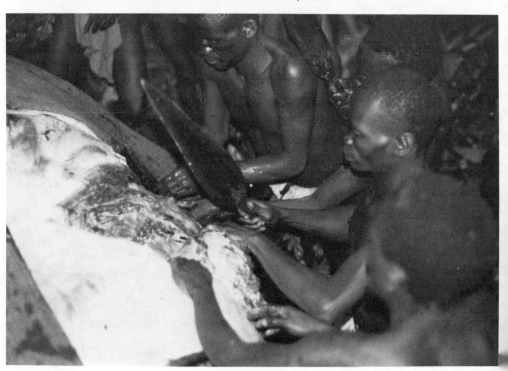

Cutting up elephant.

Dance celebrating elephant kill. Some meat is in baskets on platform around which dances move in circles.

Cutting off elephant's tail,
symbol of victory and ownership.

Kevin Duffy with Mbuti mother and child.

ominous sound of thunder approaching from the east.

To help guide the missing hunters through the darkness, Ndeke from time to time shouted loudly into the forest. "Where are you? . . . We are waiting here!" But each time there was no reply. Then the rain came and we crouched over the fires in our huts, each one of us undoubtedly wondering in his own way how Arumbu, Sukali, and Mapoli were getting along. Had they killed an elephant? Perhaps the rain had extinguished their fire. Did they have time to build even a rough shelter?

Alita and Ndasu sat in my hut taking turns feeding the fire with sticks. It would be about nine hours before dawn, and for Ndasu it was the first time since her marriage that she had been separated from Sukali for so long.

It was not until about eleven o'clock the next morning that a shout was heard in the forest. Immediately everybody recognized Sukali's voice, and I joined those who rushed to meet him. He was tired and hungry but proud of his good news.

"Arumbu speared a big elephant yesterday," he told us triumphantly. "The wound was deep and it will die soon, perhaps today, because we found blood in its tracks." Sukali held out the stick he carried. "Its tusks are as long as this," he exclaimed, standing one end of the stick on the ground so that the other came up to his shoulder. Everybody watched in fascination then as he reenacted the stalking and actual spearing of the forest giant, which we all knew could have so easily killed the hunters instead.

Apparently Arumbu had approached the big male alone, and with great stealth had thrust his spear once deeply into its belly where there were no bones to impede the blade. Then he had quickly sprinted away through the trees to rejoin Sukali and Mapoli, who were watching from a distance. Together they later found the spear where it had been torn out of the fleeing beast by the undergrowth.

It was the same technique used by the Mbuti hunter Sangu, who killed an elephant in my film *Pygmies of the Rain Forest*. I have yet to find any African Pygmy who knows of any other way to kill an elephant. The stories of spear-wielding Pygmies attacking elephants by hacking away at their rear leg tendons are difficult to believe by anybody who has hunted elephants, unless the method was meant to bring down an animal that was already immobilized because of illness or a previous injury. Pygmies I have asked about this thought such an idea to be silly and dangerous.

An elephant's leg is one of four massive columns of bone, muscle, and sinew encased in a protective skin tougher and thicker than leather. Enormous though it is, this animal can run at least as fast as a man and is not likely just to stand around in the presence of danger. It will either attack in a great rage or run off instantly. Having very poor eyesight, it may not visually detect a man's presence, even at a short distance, especially if the man is not moving. But the beast's sense of hearing is acute and its sense of smell even more so. One hunter on his own has an infinitely better chance of getting to within spearing distance than one accompanied by others. And then he has only a second of time for a single thrust of his spear into the abdomen, the one area where it will not be deflected or stopped by a bone.

In European folklore the Pygmy elephant hunter's specific anatomical target is the bladder, but this is not so in real life. I have questioned several Mbuti hunters who have killed elephants, and their only intention was simply to thrust their spears into the abdomen as far as they could so that it would do the most damage. If bleeding occurs, they believe the wound is particularly severe.

Within an hour everybody was ready to abandon the camp and migrate in the direction of the wounded elephant. Sukali had ravenously eaten a meal saved for him by Ndasu and now appeared rested enough to lead the way.

We had walked for about two hours when we came to a river over which a tall tree had fallen to form a natural bridge. It had been raining heavily and the water was flowing deep and fast. Following Sukali up onto the fallen tree I soon realized that it had been lying across the water for a long time. It was so decayed that my shoes left footprints, and pieces of rotten wood fell off to be swirled away in the water below. Balancing precariously,

I looked over my shoulder and saw that Mangoma and Asumali had already led others onto the tree behind me. I began to hurry across, but just then there was a loud cracking noise and the tree broke in the middle, tumbling us all into the water.

The water was not as deep as it looked, and I soon found that I could touch the muddy bottom with my feet. I pulled a terrified child to the bank and looked around for anybody else in trouble. But the others who had fallen in with me had floated downstream and managed to grab overhanging foliage and pull themselves to safety.

I found my shoulder bag with its damaged zip fastener where it lay half-submerged downstream against a fallen branch. My camera and the roll of film it contained were ruined. Several rolls of exposed film had floated away never to be seen again. I was thankful that at least my notebooks, which were in the pack that Sukali carried, were intact, even if somewhat damp.

With a directional precision of which I was probably the only admirer, Sukali at last led us to Arumbu and Mapoli. Near a stream, they had built a crude shelter of sticks and leaves for protection against the rain, and that was where the entire band made camp.

The hunters had followed the wounded elephant beyond this point and by now knew from certain signs that it would soon die. It was still bleeding, and they could see from its weaving tracks that it was becoming weakened and confused. Instead of fleeing directly away from its tormentors, it was blundering in a wide circle, and in its trail they found small trees that had been needlessly pushed to the ground. Then it had stopped running and turned to face its pursuers.

Arumbu was not foolish enough to close in on the wounded animal while it was still easily capable of killing him. Instead, the three hunters moved back to a stream they had recently crossed, and from there Sukali was sent to camp to bring the others.

Now the band was assembled and ready to set up camp around the elephant when and where it died. In the meantime, temporary shelters were built while we waited, and fires were made to cook some mushrooms and a small mboloko that had been collected along the way.

After Arumbu had eaten, I joined him and the other hunters to check on the elephant. It had wandered some distance from where he had last seen it, but Arumbu had little difficulty in following its tracks.

It was Sukali who saw it first. He made a clicking noise and stopped to point ahead through the trees. Then I saw it too. What looked like a dull gray rock was slowly flapping its ears in the oppressive afternoon heat. When its ears stopped moving and the tip of its trunk was raised to search the air currents, I knew that this great bull elephant had probably detected our presence.

Arumbu let a trickle of mossy material fall from his hand, and we watched as it gently floated downward but slightly in the direction of the elephant. Quickly, without noise, we changed our position until another test showed that the air was not drifting from us to the elephant. I had been in such a situation many times before, but usually with a rifle. If the animal suddenly charged, we would be quite defenseless, for Arumbu's spear was of little use in a frontal attack.

Arumbu looked up at the treetops when thunder exploded not far away. It was not a good moment for a rainstorm, and I could see that he was worried. Placing the sharp edge of his spear against his lips, he exhaled so that his breath was divided and diverted by the broad blade. Then he waved his spear in the direction in which he wanted the storm to pass, and that is what it eventually did. He believed his breath represented the storm, and that the spear blade symbolized his own presence standing in the forest as the storm passed him by on command.

Then, having diverted the storm, Arumbu decided to chance that the elephant was too weak to charge. Picking up a stick, he threw it like a spear toward the silent animal and at the same time he gave a loud yell.

When the elephant continued standing in exactly the same position, I knew, as did the other men, that it probably would never go anywhere again. If it lay down now, its great weight and weakened condition would preclude any chance of its ever regaining its feet.

When Arumbu began to move in on the stricken beast, I did not think of his action as mere bravado. The people of his hungry band were waiting between camps and did not yet know where they would sleep that night. Once the elephant was down, they would have something to eat, and they would camp near where the animal fell for as long as the meat lasted.

I stood and watched as Arumbu crept closer to the elephant, until finally he was near enough to spear it once more. But then he saw that the doomed creature was swaying unsteadily and seemed about to collapse. He jabbed it lightly with his spear and did not seem surprised when the beast failed to react. Then, with the fearlessness of an Mbuti hunter, he began to push one of the elephant's rear legs in a playful attempt to push it over. "Come," he shouted to us, "this animal is dead!"

For a moment the sound seemed to bring the animal out of its apparent stupor, and it weakly attempted to reach around toward Arumbu with its deadly trunk. But an elephant has no neck, and its trunk was not long enough to reach the man creature pushing its leg. It tottered forward a couple of steps and immediately stopped, swaying even more unsteadily.

By now the other hunters and I had joined Arumbu, and together we pushed the elephant hard each time it swayed away from us until it fell over with a resounding crash that echoed through the forest. For several minutes it breathed laboriously, and Arumbu stood ready with his spear, although he was aware there was no place he could inflict an immediate death wound with such a weapon. Then, with a great sigh the magnificent monster died. Its enormous penis, normally enclosed in its body, slid slowly out of its sheath onto the ground. A muscle in its leg twitched for a moment and then all was still.

Even Arumbu was awed by what he had done. He carefully approached the elephant's head and touched its open eye with the point of his spear and saw that it did not blink. "Now," he said quietly, "the elephant is completely dead—forever."

Only then did the hunters joyously begin to shout and dance

around the slain animal. The solemn moment of death and the dangers that led to it were soon forgotten in the elation that followed. Excitedly, they examined the uppermost tusk and compared its length against their arms. They were especially fascinated with the trunk. They knew that an elephant kills with this powerful nose, and they delighted now in touching it and dragging it back and forth with impunity.

It was Arumbu's privilege to be the first one to climb up onto the highest part of the fallen elephant in a supreme moment of triumph. Being a Pygmy, he made the giant he had killed seem even larger than it was. He stood there on the mountain of still-warm flesh and turned toward the women and children waiting off in the forest.

"Come, come, come!" he yelled at the top of his voice. "The elephant is dead! We are here. Come. The elephant is dead. Come for the feast. Come for the dancing and singing!"

He knew that the women were too far away to hear. Yet this hardly mattered, for Arumbu was performing a jubilant ritual probably unchanged since early man discovered that he could kill animals larger than himself. It was a remarkable, hair-raising scene: the diminutive hunter dancing and proclaiming his victory atop the giant elephant he had brought down single-handedly against odds that would be considered suicidal for a modern man. But Arumbu was more than a prehistoric hunter. As an Mbuti, he was also communicating with the forest itself, telling it that its children were happy once again, that they were grateful for its benevolence.

Modern men armed with powerful long-range rifles have been killed by the elephants they hunted. Yet Arumbu, the little Mbuti Pygmy, had tackled his elephant armed only with a hand-held spear, and he did it not for the useless tusks, but for the meat, so that his people would have food.

Climbing down to join the other hunters, Arumbu used his spear to cut off the tip of the elephant's trunk. When dried, this rare trophy with its twin holes would become an amulet or good-luck charm to be worn around the neck, probably by someone other than Arumbu himself.

It was Sukali who cut off the end of the elephant's tail, which contained the thick hairs commonly made into bracelets. Possession of this special symbol of victory was also proof of ownership of the kill. Sukali gave the tail to Arumbu, who was sitting on the elephant's leg.

Silently, the hunter gazed at the tail in his hand, perhaps remembering the moments when he had gambled his life and won. He handed it back to Sukali.

"Here," he said quietly, "take it to the camp so that they will know the elephant is dead."

# 9

## The Meat Festival

The women arrived the next morning and immediately began to build a new camp around the dead elephant. Fires were made and wooden racks were placed above them on poles to smoke-dry the meat when it became available. By noon, at least two other Mbuti bands had arrived to join this festival of meat.

Soon every family had their new hut built, and at last it was time for the ritual of cutting up the elephant. Already it was beginning to swell up with gas and to smell unpleasantly. Assisted by other hunters, Arumbu cut and peeled away most of the thick skin covering the huge animal's belly, exposing the bulging, white membrane that held the intestines.

In a book I have read, that included a description of the Mbuti Pygmies cutting up an elephant, it was said that "a small child is held up to bite through the membrane. A fetid explosion follows. . . ."

The "fetid explosion" is accurate enough, but no Mbuti Pygmy—or anyone else I know of—would subject a child to such abuse. Arumbu did what any Mbuti hunter would do. He carefully cut through the membrane with his spear until a thick loop of bulging intestine burst through. Then, standing well back, he reached out and punctured the loop with his spear.

Arumbu was unable to avoid a spray of foul-smelling liquid that shot from the dead animal, splattering his face and chest. For perhaps a minute, there was the sound of escaping gas before the hunters swarmed in with their knives to begin the frenetic butchering that followed.

While custom decrees that certain persons are entitled to selected parts of the elephant, the age-old axiom that possession is nine-tenths of the law applies in the Ituri just as it does elsewhere. One man wielded an ax in unfair competition with those who merely possessed knives and spears. Bloodied blades of all shapes and sizes flailed with such abandonment that it seemed there would be serious injury.

The women did not take a direct part in cutting up the carcass. They stood near their husbands, receiving pieces of meat, which they put in ever-growing piles on the ground beside them. From there the meat would eventually be transferred to the smoke racks above the fires to be cured and dried.

The most important moment of my day came when Arumbu, assisted by Sukali, dragged the elephant's trunk over to my hut and politely offered it to me as my share of the meat. I thanked him sincerely, well aware that to receive this boneless delicacy was a great honor and privilege. I did not tell him that I would rather have had a piece of meat that did not have two nostril holes running all the way through it.

That evening all three bands joined together in a continuous celebration of singing and dancing. There were songs thanking the forest for its bountifulness, and there were songs that began spontaneously out of the naturally exuberant Mbuti character. With the crowd providing a happy chorus between his im-promptu words, Arumbu sang a song in which he told of his encounter with the elephant: how he tracked it down, how the animal behaved, how he stalked it and thrust in his spear to inflict a mortal wound, and how—here he used the most graphic manner possible—the great beast finally died the next day.

Later Arumbu performed a dance in which he played the part

of the hunter, and Sukali played the part of the elephant. The crowd followed every action with the greatest interest and enjoyment, for they knew that these two men were not just play-acting, but repeating what they had actually seen and done themselves. Yet, although Arumbu was undeniably the hero of the hour, he did not occupy a special place of honor, nor did he receive any special treatment. An elephant had been killed, and he happened to be the one who killed it. This was appreciated and acknowledged by those present, yet the meat was considered a gift from the forest and would be shared among any relatives who arrived in time for the butchering and general festivities.

During the early evening, most of the dancing followed a predictable pattern, with the men and women circling the drummer counterclockwise in two separate lines, the men on the inside and the women on the outside. But as the evening advanced, it became apparent that there was some competition among the bands to show off more daring techniques.

From the edge of the forest two separate lines of men and women appeared, the men acting as women, and the women pretending to be men. It was a ritual that, in a seemingly perverse or comical way, dramatized the division of the sexes. For a brief period in time, the men did everything they could to emphasize their womanliness, even to tying breastlike objects on their chests, while the women would have delighted even the most demanding choreographers in their realistic portrayals of men.

To further exaggerate their temporary male roles, the women put objects in their bark cloths to simulate bulging male genitalia, which swung heavily from side to side as they danced. From time to time a couple would move into the center of the circle and, in their reversed roles, realistically simulate copulation to the noisy acclaim of the other dancers and of the onlookers, who included older people and children. Many sexual positions were graphically demonstrated, with the most acrobatic and imaginative actions being greeted with the loudest laughter and appreciation from everybody present.

In their public entertainment for all ages, the Mbuti see nothing wrong or immoral with the depiction of copulation as representing a natural pleasure to be openly appreciated and enjoyed. In their sense of values, it is accepted just as Western society accepts violence and killing in organized entertainment that has extended from the earliest Greek plays to modern cinema and television. An outstanding difference between our moral attitudes is that the Mbuti look on any form of violence between one person and another with great abhorrence and distaste, and never represent it in their dancing or playacting.

In the darkness beyond the dancing, I could see the fires where each family would sleep and where their meat was drying. Nearby lay all that was left of the elephant. It was not yet completely demolished and seemed to move grotesquely in the shadows of the flickering fires. The thousands of hungry flies that had been present all day did not leave the carcass when darkness came, but persisted in their eating and egg-laying all through the night. I could still clearly hear their constant, ominous drone from my hut after the dancing had stopped and everybody had gone to sleep.

Within a couple of days, the scene around the elephant resembled a miniature battlefield, with bloodied pieces of skin, bone, and intestine lying everywhere. Each of the three bands had made their camps slightly apart, and greetings and conversations between them were shouted in cheerful good humor. It was a time for greeting old acquaintances and for the teenagers to seek out exciting new friends and possibly even future wives and husbands.

The smell of the scattered remains of the elephant was getting worse, but nobody seemed to care. A group of young girls was skipping rope, using a piece of liana. Their agility was extraordinary, and their happy laughter seemed to set the mood for everyone else.

Sukali and Mapoli were part of a group of younger hunters who were demonstrating their incredible skill as archers. Somebody would throw a banana high in the air and the others would shoot arrows at it. The one whose arrow pierced the fruit received it as a reward. More than once the banana was struck by two arrows simultaneously and then it was divided in half for the winners.

When somebody dragged a great length of vine into camp, it was the signal for everyone to stop whatever they were doing and playfully join in a hectic tug-of-war, with the men pulling one end and the women pulling the other. This was more a game for adults, and the younger children watched from a distance to avoid being trampled as both sides dug in their heels and screamed encouragement to their fellows. There were no fixed rules, and when one side seemed to be losing ground, some of their teammates would run to those pulling on the other end and attack them so that they lost their grip on the rope. It seemed exceedingly important to win, but at no time did it become more than a hilarious game, especially when one side lost and collapsed in a tangled, laughing heap on the ground. The men and women won about the same number of times before everybody eventually wandered off to check how their meat was drying, or whatever else demanded their attention at the moment.

I was chatting with Sukali about our going together to the forest place called Apalura when he suddenly gave a knowing smile over my shoulder. I looked around and saw Mapoli nonchalantly leading an attractive girl into the forest. The never reticent Sukali soon brought me up to date on this latest camp romance. Mapoli was Sukali's younger brother and he had recently come to believe that he should have a wife of his own. When Mapoli met Mabili, a girl of about fourteen from one of the other bands, it was apparently love at first sight, or perhaps second sight. Since last meeting her, she had reached puberty and was now a museka and eligible for the pleasurable activity of arobo, or free love—and eventual marriage.

Mabili was a tall girl for an Mbuti, with darker skin than most of her clan. Her face was almost haughty for one so young and she seldom smiled. But when she finally did, for Mapoli, his heart was won. According to Sukali, his brother had found the girl of his dreams, and she had agreed to be his wife. But for Mapoli there would be a major obstacle to overcome.

Among the various village tribes of the Ituri, and indeed throughout much of tropical Africa, a young man obtains a wife by paying a bridal price to her parents. This may consist of livestock and cash or goods, or even a commitment to work for his parents-in-law for a year or more. But livestock and material goods do not have the same value to the Mbuti who, as nomads, cannot accumulate them and become wealthy. More importantly, however, because every young woman in an Mbuti band is critical to its survival, the band demands that she be replaced by another marriageable girl if somebody from another band wants to marry her.

In this case, it happened that there was a young man in Mabili's band who also wanted a wife. In order to satisfy all parties concerned, Mapoli would have to find a girl in his own band whom he could offer in exchange for Mabili. But he was luckier than some prospective husbands, for his cousin Manjahi finally decided that she liked the other young man and agreed to marry him. Such a system of "sister exchange" serves the nomadic Mbuti well in helping to maintain the integrity of the band. Serious rows can result between bands if it is not applied fairly, or if the couple elopes because there is no "sister" available for exchange.

Traditionally, Mapoli would also have to kill an antelope and lay it on the ground before Mabili's father, hoping to receive his blessing—and his daughter. If and when the father agreed, the young couple would be considered married without further ceremony. There would be no written record of the event, and the day, month, and year would not be remembered, because they were never known. That same night they would sleep together in their new hut, and from then on both would be responsible for doing their parts in perpetuating the husband's band.

There is one other ritual preceding marriage, which is actually a formal celebration and public recognition of an Mbuti girl's first flow of menstrual blood. Such a rite of passage, or initiation into womanhood, is sometimes delayed until two or more eligible girls become available to make a big celebration worthwhile. Then it becomes a festival that the Efe Mbuti call *Pepa* and other Mbuti call *Elima*. Among the Efe, it often takes place at a roadside village when more than one band may be camping together.

The teenage initiates and their younger and older girlfriends occupy a special enlarged Pepa hut for many days, during which time they are instructed by older women in the ways of marriage, including explicit advice on how to sexually please a man. Much of the instruction, however, involves teaching the girls the lovely Pepa songs, which are sung at no other time.

In her book *Eight Years with Congo Pigmies* (1954), Ann Putnam describes witnessing such an event (at Epulu), which she called "Alima." As the wife of Patrick Putnam, mentioned earlier, she was able to see the festivities from beginning to end and wrote about them in some detail. Colin Turnbull, in writing about this festival (*The Forest People*, 1961), said, "For the Pygmies the elima is one of the happiest, most joyful occasions in their lives."

In an earlier book, *Black Elephant Hunter* (1960), I described the girls' initiation ceremonies of the Bemba and Bisa tribes in Zambia, among whom I lived and worked for many years. There the event is called *Cisungu*, or *Mbusa* among the Bisa people, and in many ways it is not unlike what occurs in the Ituri.

The more dramatic parts of the Mbuti version include the right of the girls to select the young men of their choice as their lovers, to invite them to the seclusion of the Pepa hut. The girls indicate their amorous preferences by leaving the hut now and then to stalk and attack their "victims" by painfully thrashing them with a whiplike stick. Anyone whipped is later obliged to run the gauntlet of older women, who are armed with sticks and whose dedicated duty it is to prevent them from reaching the seductive girls, who by then are waiting expectantly in the hut.

The young men who attempt to reach the girls in the hut may include those who have not been whipped but who also want to prove their manhood while having a good time. If a boy or man can ignore the pain the women guardians inflict and reaches a girl in the hut, there are no restrictions on what the young couple may do together.

The Mbuti are known for their unpredictability and for their sometimes volatile change of moods. Out of the tranquility of one sunny morning a particularly stormy row flared up more suddenly than a tropical thunderstorm. It happened when some children apparently bumped against the meat rack over Asumali's fire. It collapsed soon afterward, throwing its heavy load to the ground, and everyone laughed when Asumali rushed to pick up his meat from the ashes and surrounding mud. Nothing infuriates an Mbuti more than being laughed at, and Asumali instantly flew into a rage.

"You!" he screamed at those laughing and at Mangoma in particular. "You allowed those children to play here and spoil my meat!" Actually, it mattered little to Asumali that his meat had fallen to the ground. What really mattered was being laughed at. Yet he turned to the one person who was not amused, his wife Matuneo, and began to beat her on the head and shoulders with his fists.

Some Mbuti women would have fought back, but Matuneo was a person as gentle as Asumali was aggressive, and she just sat there, her face showing more sadness than fear or pain. She did not move when Asumali then turned to their hut and in a terrible frenzy began to tear it out of the ground stick by stick until their simple home was totally destroyed. Then he rushed over to Mangoma.

"This is not a good place for people!" he yelled. "It's only good for animals!"

With that he helped Matuneo put their meat in their basket and together they disappeared into the forest in the direction of Kulani, a Lese village that lay near the road. Their daughter, Maguti, and their youngest son, Afilobo, trailed along behind them, carrying whatever family possessions and meat that could not be put in their mother's basket.

Sukali watched his parents depart and shrugged. "We'll see

them tomorrow when we go to Kulani," he told me. "There in the village," he added with a broad smile, "there will be much beer and food—and many girls!"

"We are leaving the forest tomorrow?"

"Yes," Sukali said. "The meat is almost dry and everybody wants to go to Kulani where the Lese are waiting for meat."

I knew that the villagers had probably known about the elephant since the day it died. That would have given them time to brew some of their potent banana beer for the feast that traditionally followed a successful elephant hunt.

"What about going with me to Apalura now?" I asked.

Sukali looked at me curiously. "Why do you want to go to Apalura?"

"It is the last day before I go to the road. I want to see the center of the forest before I leave."

Sukali thought about it quietly for a moment and then jumped to his feet with sudden enthusiasm. "Let's go," he exclaimed. "It's a long way and we must leave now or we won't have time to return here by tonight." Ndasu and Alita were sitting nearby and he shouted at them to come with us, and a few minutes later we were all on our way.

It was a fine, sunny day and we walked quickly for perhaps two hours until Sukali began to slow down and to lower his voice as if afraid that it might be heard by someone or something ahead. "Now we are near Apalura, the center of the forest," he whispered, "the place where God lives."

Both girls caught up with us and stayed close as we continued forward. Then Sukali stopped.

"Let's go back," he said. "It's getting late."

"No," I pleaded. "Let's go just a little farther and see the cave."

Sukali stood his ground. "That is the place where Tore stays with the spirits of the dead," he warned. "And there is a great snake which guards everything for Tore."

"Do you know of anybody who has been harmed or killed there?"

"No," Sukali muttered doubtfully.

"Then, if you're not too frightened, let's go and see this place," I said.

Sukali looked from Ndasu and Alita back to me, then took an iron-tipped arrow from his quiver and held it ready to place against his bowstring at an instant's notice. He began to walk forward and we followed.

We were on the bank of a small river, which at that point went between two hills. The canopy above then became so dense that the sky was completely obscured and we found ourselves enveloped in an eerie darkness. A small cliff reared up from the water's edge and through the gloom I could see a cave.

Sukali stopped and silently pointed at the dark opening. "That's it, the cave where Tore lives!" he whispered.

"Can we go inside?" I whispered back.

Sukali looked at me as if I were crazy. "No," he said emphatically. "No one can go inside!"

The two girls were staring at the cave, and they both looked as if they were ready to run back the way they had come. It was cold and damp in this dark place where the sun never shone. Alita shivered and I could see goose bumps all over her nearly naked body. The only sound was the trickling of water as it flowed past our feet.

I looked around me at this place they said was the home of Tore and his spirits of the dead and wondered if Ndima was watching us now as an invisible Lodi. Sukali may have had similar thoughts, for suddenly he said, "Let's go!" and without looking to see if we followed, he abruptly walked off downstream. We hurried after him and soon the canopy above us became less dense as friendly shafts of sunlight began to dispel the chill and brighten up the forest around us.

Then the river meandered into a picturesque glade so breathtaking in its beauty that I stopped in my tracks. Hundreds of butterflies, which normally would have been found high in the canopy above the floor of the forest, were clustered on the damp sand of a little island in the middle of the river.

"This," Sukali said with a touch of pride, "is Apalura, the most beautiful place in the forest!"

"But I thought the place with the cave was Apalura," I said.

"Yes, it is," Sukali explained, "but it is a different part of Apalura. Tore lives in the cave, and this is where God lives!" Then he glanced mischievously at Ndasu. "Before we became married," he said with a grin, "the camps of our parents were near this place and we came here often to make love on the island, and sometimes in the river itself!" With that, he gleefully chased Ndasu through the shallow water to catch her somewhere among the bushes on the other bank. The moments of pleasure in a lifelong struggle to survive in the forest are fleeting, and the Mbuti celebrate them with a passion probably unequaled by any other people on earth. And besides, it seemed that making love in the warm, bright light of day beside a secluded stream was more romantic than in the gloomy interior of an Mbuti hut at night, especially when it's surrounded by other little huts with hear-through walls, all occupied by gossipy neighbors who are quite likely to provide a loud, running commentary on one's amorous activities.

This was to be my last day in the forest, for I knew we would all leave for the road the next morning. I had first become closely acquainted with Alita in circumstances not unlike the present, and as with Sukali and Ndasu, it was a sentimental moment that could not easily be ignored.

If Ndima, along with a host of other long dead Mbuti, was watching us, I somehow knew his thoughts would be kind and favorable. For I too loved the forest and everything in it. I could never be an Mbuti, yet for a time I had been granted the privilege of being welcomed as one of their own.

It was the morning of our departure from the forest, and there was to be a final dance for this special occasion. The Mbuti believe that the forest hears their music and listens to their songs. The elephant had provided more meat than a hundred tiny mboloko antelope, and now with song and dance the people communed with and thanked their forest—the forest they have loved and venerated since the misty beginnings of time. They wore clusters of green leaves tucked into their belts, and some of the men played little bamboo flutes as they danced. These things and everything else they possessed were of the forest, even as they themselves were of the forest.

One of the hunters then appeared with a bloodied tusk held under each of his muscular arms. Crouching down in imitation of an elephant, he dashed among the huts, scattering parts of them in all directions with the tips of the tusks. Unable to resist, other hunters followed in pursuit until after a long stalk and several exciting encounters they brought the "elephant" down with imaginary spear thrusts. As he lay dying and thrashing about in a most realistic manner, one hunter pretended to cut off his tail—a small leafy branch, which he held high for all to see.

Arumbu did not take part in these events but sat quietly with some of his friends. He had done his part in killing the elephant, and except for that first night of singing and dancing, he did not talk about it. It was enough that the people were happy and would be eating elephant meat for weeks to come. His owner in the village would be pleased with his share, which included most of the trunk that I had diplomatically returned rather than see it wasted. Once in the village, Arumbu could take almost anything he wanted—anything except a village girl. Even the killing of an elephant was not important enough to break such a social taboo. Otherwise, when the Mbuti arrived with the meat, they would be allowed the run of the village for several days.

During this time they would expect to take or be given whatever they wanted—beer, juicy pineapples, sweet potatoes, cassava, bananas—all the cultivated foods they like to eat. In return the villagers would receive the meat they craved. In this respect, the villagers are much the same as people elsewhere who like meat and potatoes except that the villagers do not generally have the meat. The opposite is true of the Mbuti, who generally do not have the potatoes.

While staying at the road, the Mbuti would be based in their own camp built near the village where they would sleep each night. During the day and evening, when they were not eating tasty, cultivated foods, they would sometimes dance for the villagers who, like the ancient Egyptians before them, think highly of such entertainment. When such dancing becomes erotic, the villagers thoroughly enjoy every suggestive movement, yet later disparagingly describe it as an example of Mbuti depravity.

Meanwhile, here in the forest the dance had just ended, and I knew that it was time to leave the place where the elephant died. The meat was dry now, and I had seen it packed into baskets and tied with bark rope into individual loads. It was no longer bloody but had assumed a dark wine color and had lost more than half its weight in the smoke and heat of the fires. I walked over to examine the skeletal remains of the elephant, but some distance from where the main butchering had taken place I found myself walking on a seething carpet of maggots so deep that they wriggled over the tops of my shoes.

We left this moving feast to the ants and the birds and departed in a straggling line on the six-hour trek to the road and, for me, to the outside world. I glanced over my shoulder and saw the smoke from an abandoned fire curling lazily upward into the tall trees, and for a few moments more I could see the fragile little huts standing forlorn and empty. Memories crowded my mind as I tried to pick out the one that had been mine. Then the scene was lost to me forever, and I hurried to catch up with those who had gone ahead.

I knew that if ever I returned, the huts would be gone, without even a building posthole to indicate they had ever existed. The thin saplings the Mbuti women drove into the ground in making their temporary shelters would leave little trace. Only the bones of the elephant would remain after a year. Then they too would gradually return to the soil. For everything taken by the Mbuti from the forest was returned to it, even the Mbuti themselves.

## Epilogue

To the Mbuti, the past is unimportant because it is gone completely and forever. As for the future, they have little desire to control what does not yet exist. The present is something that happens every day, and is to be enjoyed with consideration for others, with love, and sometimes with passion.

The Mbuti's natural and total harmony with their ecosystem is something from which all people can learn. Their innate gentleness, their music, dance, and song, a rich folklore, their mastery of a complex environment—these things reflect *their* kind of civilization, one so successful that it may have lasted longer than any other on earth. They were highly esteemed by the ancient Egyptians and immortalized by Homer, Herodotus, and Aristotle. They were around when the Magna Carta was signed in 1215 and when Columbus "discovered" America in 1492. They were there to guide Stanley in the nineteenth century and may well have saved him from starvation and death. Somehow the diminutive hunters and gatherers survived down through the ages, but for how long?

Today the Mbuti's carefree, nomadic ways are rapidly ending

with the inexorable and pervasive intrusion of the twentieth century. The original inhabitants of the Ituri have been instructed by the authority of a distant government to settle permanently in villages along the road, where they can be counted and pay taxes.

There will be no known date, no witnesses, and no fanfare when, in the name of progress, the last Mbuti nomad finally leaves the forest. When he does, an entire people will be gone forever, and there will be none like them to take their place. The vast interior of the great forest, which may have been the birthplace of mankind itself, will be empty of laughter, dance, and song for the first time since human life there began. A natural way of living that all people once knew in an innocent age will have vanished from the face of the earth as the Mbuti pass into history.

We should remember them well, for the Mbuti mirror our past. They are the living spirits of our not so distant hunting and gathering ancestors.